Fred Wilson

SIMPLE ATTACKING PLANS

MONGOOSE
Press

Publisher: Mongoose Press
1005 Boylston Street, Suite 324
Newton Highlands, MA 02461
info@mongoosepress.com
www.MongoosePress.com

ISBN 978-1-9362774-38
Library of Congress Control Number: 2012949221

Distributed to the trade by National Book Network
custserv@nbnbooks.com, 800-462-6420
For all other sales inquiries please contact the publisher.

Editor: Jorge Amador
Layout: Andrey Elkov
Cover Design: Kaloyan Nachev
Printed in the United States of America

First English edition
0 9 8 7 6 5 4 3 2

ACKNOWLEDGEMENTS

Special thanks to Maya Chase, Sandra Cotuna, Noreen Davisson, Glen Hart, Jeffrey Tannenbaum, and Rita Kelly for the many valuable suggestions, tremendous support and great patience they all displayed while helping me to create this book.

TABLE OF CONTENTS

MORE SELECTED GAMES

DEFLECTION, UNDERMINING,
OR REMOVING THE GUARD? 160

INTRODUCTION

Methodical thinking is of more use in Chess than inspiration.
—C.J.S. Purdy

You don't need to plan if you can afford to fail.
—Bruce Pandolfini

Opportunity is missed by most chessplayers because it looks like work.
—with apologies to Thomas Edison

This book is primarily for those players who "don't know what they are doing or why" ...but would like to learn! If you have been playing chess for a while now, think you do have some talent for the game, but frequently mess up what are clearly very good – or even winning – positions, then read on. I'd even like to think that you have opened this book because you have finally realized *chess is not just a random series of tactical opportunities,* and are really ready to learn some fundamental aggressive plans. In other words, you are sick and tired of having to reinvent the wheel every time you play!

In my more than thirty years of both playing and teaching chess, during which time I have achieved a master rating in both slow (tournament) and fast chess, I have come to believe that there are only four essential, even primitive, concepts which you must learn and understand in order to play successful attacking chess. These are:

- In the opening, whenever justified, relentlessly attack the weak squares f7 or f2.

- Most successful kingside attacks are directed against the squares h7 or h2, and they are often preceded by eliminating or driving off its defender.

- If your opponent's king is trapped in the center, make every reasonable effort to open and dominate the *e-file*, and sometimes the *d-file* also!

- If possible, point all your pieces at your opponent's king!

Okay, I know you may not always be able to use all of your pieces during an attack, but you get the idea – use as many as possible. After all, if your attackers outnumber the defenders, doesn't it make sense that superior force should win?

Consider the following four examples of how these attacking ideas look in action.

1. Scotch Game
Richard Davisson – Michael Perlowitz
U.S. Amateur Championship East 2008

1. e4	e5
2. ♘f3	♘c6
3. d4	f6?

A logical-looking but awful move often made by inexperienced players. Besides opening the a2-g8 diagonal, which may make it harder for Black to castle, it also takes away the best square for Black's king knight. As a general rule of thumb, *in all double king pawn (1. e4 e5) openings, when White plays an early d2-d4 Black should always trade pawns if White cannot recapture with a pawn.*

4. ♗c4!   ♗e7??

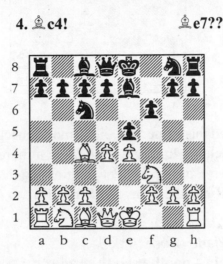

Not obviously a blunder, and even a well-intentioned move. I believe Black was worried about 5. dxe5 fxe5 6. ♘g5, which would now lose a piece. But while 4...d6 was playable, 4...♗e7?? is a terrible mistake. Why?

5. dxe5!   fxe5
6. ♕d5!   ...

Hitting f7 where it hurts! White, a strong scholastic player, foresaw that Black now has no acceptable way of defending f7, and expected 6...♘h6 7. ♗xh6 ♖f8 8. ♗xg7 with an easily won position. Instead he was pleasantly surprised by ...

6. ...   d6??
7. ♕f7+   ♔d7
8. ♗e6!#

9

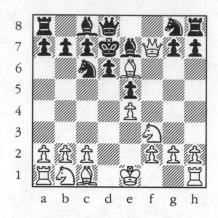

I have dubbed this game "the eight-move checkmate" and often use it when teaching. Rarely will you see a more devastating example of a queen + bishop *battery* dominating the f7 square in the opening. Still, Richard did have to *know what to look for*.

2. Giuoco Piano ("fork trick")
John Whately – another sixth-grader
Public School 9 Tournament New York 1999

1. e4		e5
2. ♘f3		♘f6
3. ♘c3		♘c6
4. ♗c4(?)		...

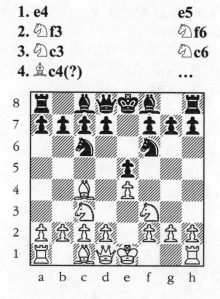

While not strictly speaking a mistake (and it is often played!), this move does allow Black complete equality by means of a simple tactical trick, and it is clearly inferior to 4. d4 or 4. ♗b5.

4. ...   ♘xe4!

This usually comes as a shock to White, who almost always reacts quickly, and badly, by playing 5. ♘xe4 d5! (the point of the "fork trick") 6. ♗xd5? (6. ♗d3 is best, so that White keeps his *bishop pair*) 6...♕xd5 with slightly better center control and the *bishop pair* for Black. Interestingly, sometimes when a talented player is surprised by the "fork trick" he will try to recover his pawn with the counter-combination 5. ♗xf7+?! ♔xf7 6. ♘xe4, though after 6...d5! 7. ♘fg5+ ♔g8 8. ♕f3 ♕d7! Black is also better.

John, a strong scholastic player at the time, did not know a lot of opening theory but, if surprised, usually really slowed down to think it through. To his credit, he found a third reasonable reply for White that I had never seen before.

5. ♗d5?!   ♘xc3

Probably, 5...♘f6! is Black's best move as after 6. ♗xc6 dxc6 7. ♘xe5 ♗c5 Black has the initiative and the two bishops.

6. dxc3   ♗c5?

6...♗e7 is safer, as it prevents any threats from White involving ♘g5. Now White can recover his pawn by 7. ♗xf7+!? if he chooses, though after 7...♔xf7 8. ♕d5+ ♔f8 9. ♕xc5+ d6 10. ♕c4 the position is unclear. Incidentally, while 7. ♘g5! leads to tremendous complications favoring White after 7...♕f6! 8. ♗xf7+ ♔f8 9. 0-0!, John's move is also good.

7. 0-0   0-0

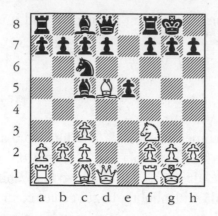

This was probably Black's best bet, although now White can initiate a strong attack. How?

8. ♘g5!   d6??

Already having played a couple of second-best moves in this game, Black (who actually was the more experienced and higher-rated junior), now commits a real "howler." Probably he thought that his opponent, who had fallen into a "book trap" and had so far refused to win his pawn back, was just a "bozo." In fact, he had to try 8...h6 9. ♘xf7 ♖xf7 10.♗xf7+ ♔xf7 11. ♕d5+, although White regains the piece with the safer king position. How did John punish Black's carelessness?

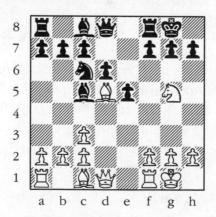

9. ♕h5!	h6 (forced)
10. ♘xf7	♖xf7
11. ♗xf7+	♔h8??

The final blunder. Black had to play 11...♔f8, although after 12. ♗d5 he is the exchange down in a poor position.

12. ♗xh6	♕f6

Children never resign.

13. ♗g5+	♕h6
14. ♗xh6	♗f5
15. ♕xf5	♖f8
16. ♗xg7+	♔xg7
17. ♕g6+	♔h8
18. ♕h6#	

Moral: never be contemptuous of your opponent!

You may have noticed that, in each of the first two games, the winning blow was a *long, strong queen move*. In fact, it is almost a corollary of my four basic attacking concepts that *most successful attacks require a long queen move*. You will see repeated examples of this for both White and Black throughout this book.

The next two games are somewhat more complex and sophisticated, as the winners are grandmasters and the losers (at the time) were international masters.

3. Sicilian Defense, Nimzowitsch Variation
B. Parma – V. Kozomara
18th Yugoslav Championship, Vrnjačka Banja 1962

1. e4	**c5**
2. ♘f3	**♘f6**

An unusual variation intended to provoke White's next move, although 3. ♘c3 is also good.

3. e5	**♘d5**
4. ♘c3	**♘xc3**
5. dxc3	**d5**

Apparently 5...♘c6 is played more often, but after 6. ♗f4 e6 7. ♕d2 ♕c7 8. 0-0-0 White has the edge as Black's position is rather cramped. So Black's last move, attempting to seize control of important center squares, certainly makes sense, and in fact White has only one move to retain some advantage. What is it?

6. exd6! **...**

Of course, the *en passant* capture is the only way to create any problems for Black. If 6...exd6, then after 7. ♗c4 White's superior development plus total control of the d5 square add up to a clear advantage.

6. ...		♛xd6
7. ♗e3!		...

Interestingly, we are already "out of book," as this position reached by reasonable moves from both sides cannot be found in either *Modern Chess Openings,* 14th Edition (1999) nor the equally encyclopedic *Nunn's Chess Openings* (1999). In fact, Nunn in a brief footnote suggests 7. ♕xd6 exd6 8. ♗f4 with an advantage for White, but clearly GM Bruno Parma took a long, hard look at this possibility and decided he wanted more. Now the ball is in Black's court regarding a queen trade, but he probably rejected it because he feared White's advantage in development after 7...♕xd1+ 8. ♖xd1 e6. Nevertheless, this was the best choice as after...

7. ...		♘c6

...White did not give him a second chance!

8. ♗d3!		e5?

This is too loosening and weakens Black's control of important

15

light squares. 8...e6 was more circumspect. Now how did White get the ball rolling?

| 9. ♘g5! | ♗e7 |

Besides knowing when it is OK to move "the same piece twice in the opening," grandmasters also know how to start an attack! How did GM Parma begin?

10. ♕h5!	g6
11. ♕h6	♗f8
12. ♕h4	♕e7
13. ♗c4!	...

Repositioning the bishop on the weakened diagonal.

13. ...	♘d8
14. 0-0-0	♗e6
15. ♗xe6	fxe6

Black's last move was forced, for 15...♘xe6?? 16. ♕a4+ loses on the spot. (Remember to *always look for that long, strong queen move!*) Still, even though Black can hardly move, his position seems to be holding together, so what plan did Parma find to achieve a breakthrough?

16. ♖d2! ...

White can crash through by simply doubling rooks on the d-file. Black's king trapped in the center has no escape.

16. ...	♞c6
17. ♖hd1	h6
18. ♕h3!	1-0

The knight is immune because Black's rook would be hanging after 18...hxg5. And if 18...♞d8, protecting e6, then 19. ♞e4!, threatening both 20. ♗xc5 and 20. ♞d6+, is crushing.

Our next example is a brilliant, very instructive, and curiously little-known attacking masterpiece against a castled king played by six-time U.S. Champion Grandmaster Walter Browne. In this game, Browne combines a couple of our basic attacking ideas with a significantly more complicated one: *sacrifices are often necessary to break up the pawn barrier protecting your opponent's king.*

4. Caro-Kann Defense, Bronstein-Larsen Variation
W. Browne – J. Bellón
Las Palmas 1977

1. e4	c6
2. d4	d5
3. ♘c3	dxe4
4. ♘xe4	♘f6
5. ♘xf6	gxf6

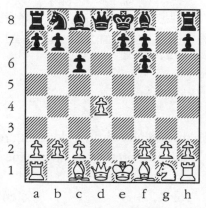

A radical variation of this normally "super-solid" defense often played in the 1950s and '60s by David Bronstein and Bent Larsen, two of the most uncompromising grandmasters of that era. Black accepts a damaged pawn structure in return for an unbalanced position where he may get some attacking chances on the g-file if White castles kingside. Modern opening theory recommends that White fianchetto his king bishop via the sequence 6. c3 ♗f5 7. ♘f3 ♕c7 8. g3 ♘d7 9. ♗g2 0-0-0 10. 0-0, when White will have the more dangerous attacking chances. Browne's idea of developing quickly with an eye towards generating early central pressure after 9. c4! is also good.

6. ♗e2	♗f5

7. ♘f3	♛c7
8. 0-0	e6
9. c4!	♘d7
10. ♗e3	...

Black's next move is a mistake as it allows White to keep him cramped with a *gain of time;* while 10...0-0-0 looks risky in view of 11. ♛a4! followed by b2-b4. Perhaps 10...♗e7 is safest.

10. ...	♗d6?
11. c5	♗e7
12. ♘d2!	...

Foreseeing an interesting attacking plan if Black castles king-side, but again if 12...0-0-0, White still has 13. ♛a4 ♚b8 14. b4 with a powerful initiative.

12. ...	0-0

So how did Browne begin his plan?

13. f4! ♗**g6**

Black's last move was forced, as White was threatening to trap the bishop with 14. g4! followed by 15. f5. Now how can White open more lines for his pieces and inflict further damage on the pawn barrier in front of Black's king?

14. f5! ♗**xf5**
15. ♖xf5! ...

This sacrifice is the only logical follow-up to White's first one and is very instructive precisely because it *cannot* be calculated to a definite conclusion! But notice that, after the next five or six moves, Browne must have looked ahead that *all White's pieces are pointing at* Black's *king and he has a ferocious initiative*. It is this ability to *correctly evaluate* positions reached by concrete calculation that separates masters from amateurs.

15. ...	exf5
16. ♗d3	♖fe8
17. ♗xf5	♘f8
18. ♘e4!	♔h8
19. ♕h5!	♘g6
20. ♖f1(?)	...

The odd-looking 20. b4! was probably stronger as it would have prevented Black's best response to 20. ♖f1, 20...♕a5!. After the necessary 21. ♘c3 (21. ♖f3 ♕e1+) 21...♕b4, Black has some diversionary counterplay.

20...	♖g8?
21. ♖f3!	♕a5??

The losing blunder; 21...♖g7 had to be played. However, after 22. ♗h6 Black must return the exchange by 22...♖ag8! with an inferior position, for if 22...♖7g8? (as pointed out by well-known New York chess teacher Sandra Notuna) then 23. ♖h3 ♕d8 (if 23...♕a5 24. ♗d2 wins) 24. ♗f8! ♕xd4+ 25. ♔h1 ♘xf8 26. ♕xh7+! and mate next move.

Now how did Browne conclude his attacking gem?

22. ♛xh7+!!   **1-0**

22...♚xh7 23. ♖h3+ ♚g7 24. ♗h6+ ♚h8 25. ♗f8+ and mate next move. This is the type of finish we all dream about – sacrificing the queen to force checkmate being the ultimate example of *mind over matter* in chess. And yet, remember how Browne achieved this: by using a largely intuitive, not fully calculable sacrifice that seriously weakened Bellón's kingside while *methodically bringing all his pieces to bear against the enemy king*. He didn't use "magic" of any kind but rather simply applied some basic attacking concepts that you, too, can learn to work with through study and practice.

It is also important to remember that while some of the incredibly strong computer chess programs available today, such as *Rybka* or *Fritz*, may have been able to survive Browne's onslaught, your opponents can't! They are not "super-grandmasters," but rather players like yourself who find it much easier to attack (or at least to try to maintain the balance) than to defend against dangerous, well-planned aggression.

What I believe you can learn by studying the annotated games in this book is how to recognize when the situation is ripe for starting a simple, basic attacking plan and how to methodically – and, yes, also creatively – implement it.

So, to very simply recapitulate the fundamental attacking ideas you will repeatedly see illustrated in this book, *in the opening* you should:

- **Always be on the lookout for "shots" against f7 or f2.**

- **Relentlessly work to open and control the e- or d-files if your opponent's king is trapped in the center.**

Whereas *in the middlegame* you should:

- **Almost always aim your kingside attacks at h7 or h2, or at the *analogous squares* on the queenside.**

- **Point all (or as many as possible) of your pieces at your opponent's king!**

And don't forget the two important corollaries to the four simple attacking plans:

- **A *long, strong queen move* is a necessary feature of many winning attacks!**

- **Sacrifices are often the only way to damage or destroy the enemy king's pawn shelter.**

I think that if you carefully go through the annotated games in this book, you will be able to introduce, with success, these basic attacking concepts into your own play. You will need to practice them consistently, without fear of making mistakes or losing. Neither should you become discouraged by the inevitable defeats caused by miscalculation or oversights. This hard work is essential in order to change your style, become a stronger, more aggressive player – and enjoy many more exciting victories than you ever had before!

Finally, if you already know how to attack you can still enjoy this book, both as a refresher course and as an entertaining collection of little-known games, several of which are truly neglected masterpieces.

Now get cracking!

—Fred Wilson, August 2012

5. Caro-Kann Defense
Nicolas Rossolimo – W.A. Winser
Hastings 1949-50

1. e4	**c6**
2. d4	**d5**
3. ♘c3	**...**

With the Caro-Kann Defense, Black stakes a claim in the center by controlling the d5 square. He is willing to remain slightly cramped throughout the opening in order to obtain a solid, seemingly safe position. However, after White's third move, 3. ♘c3 (or 3. ♘d2), Black's best move is to capture the e4-pawn as there is no good alternative: both 3...e6 and 3...♘f6 4. e5 leave Black with an inferior version of the French Defense. So, for a while White will have more center control.

3. ...	**dxe4**
4. ♘xe4	**...**

25

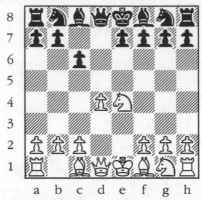

Black is at a crossroads; he must now decide how to develop his minor pieces. The two most common continuations today are 4...♗f5 5. ♘g3 ♗g6, called the Classical Variation, and 4...♘d7, known as the Smyslov Variation, in honor of the former world champion who played it often. The purpose of 4...♘d7 is to play his other knight to f6 to trade off White's strongly centralized knight on e4. If White trades knights, Black simply recaptures with his knight, not only avoiding doubled pawns, but retaining a knight on f6 (usually his most important defensive minor piece in any opening).

4. ...	**♘d7**
5. ♘f3	**♘gf6**
6. ♘xf6+	**♘xf6**
7. ♘e5	**...**

An interesting move – later favored by another world champion, Anatoly Karpov – whose chief purpose is to discourage Black from developing his light-squared bishop. After 7...♗f5 8. c3 e6 9. g4! ♗g6 10. h4, Black has problems. While the awkward-looking 7...♗e6 has occasionally been played here, probably Black's safest move is 7...♘d7 aiming to exchange or drive off White's active knight. Black's reply in this game is a bit passive and it locks in his light-squared bishop.

| 7. ... | e6 |
| 8. ♗d3 | ... |

Huh? Can't Black capture the unprotected d4-pawn? OK, clearly *Grandmaster* Rossolimo is not hanging a pawn on move 8, nor did the British master Winser "fall for it." If 8...♕xd4? 9. ♘xf7! ruining Black's position, as 9...♔xf7 fails to 10. ♗g6+ winning the queen via a *discovered attack*.

8. ...	♗d6
9. 0-0	♕c7
10. ♖e1	b6

Black is reluctant to castle because after 11. ♗g5 White has a strong kingside attack in the making.

| 11. ♕f3 | ♗b7 |
| 12. ♗g5! | ... |

A complicated position in which Black's decision not to play 12...c5, with a discovered attack on White's queen, requires a detailed explanation. It seems Rossolimo analyzed this possibility and thought that 12... c5 13. ♗b5+ ♔f8 (13...♔e7 14. ♗c6! ♗xc6 15. ♘xc6+ with a tremendous attack) 14. ♕h3?! cxd4 15. ♗xf6 gxf6 16. ♕h6+ ♔e7 17. ♘d7! ♗e5 18. ♖xe5! fxe5 19. ♕f6+ wins. However, *Fritz* 10 says that Black is better after 14. ♕h3 ♘e4!. It recommends 13. ♕h3 and rates White as a bit better here. Sometimes there is no substitute for hard, concrete analysis, both during and *after* the game!

12. ...	♗e7
13. ♖ad1	♖c8
14. c3	h6
15. ♕h3!	...

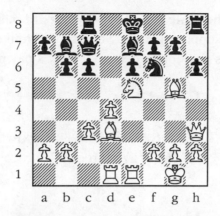

Not only indirectly protecting the attacked bishop, but also getting his queen into position to begin a winning sacrificial attack. Notice how all six of White's major and minor pieces are participating in the assault. Now Black is afraid to castle because White would have a powerful sacrifice with 15. ♗xh6. Nor can he relieve his position through exchanges by 15…♘d5 because of 16. ♗xe7 ♕xe7 17. ♘g6! fxg6 18. ♖xe6.

15. …   ♗d6

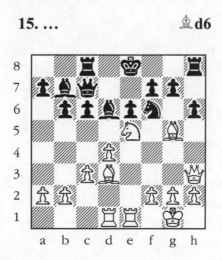

Now everything is in place for a standard sacrificial breakthrough. Black's king is trapped in the center; White has enormous pressure down the e-file and all his pieces are putting pressure on squares near the opposing king. So, can you find the combination White has in this position to destroy Black's pawn barrier?

16. ♘xf7!		♛xf7

If 16...♚xf7 17. ♕xe6+ ♚f8 18. ♗xf6 gxf6 19. ♕xf6+ ♚g8 20. ♗c4+ ♚h7 21. ♖e6! ♕g7 (forced) 22. ♕f5+ and mate next move.

17. ♖xe6+		♗e7
18. ♗xf6		gxf6
19. ♖de1		...

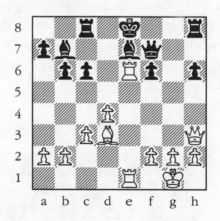

Here Black chose to give up his queen for two rooks, but why not 19...♖c7 protecting the pinned bishop? Take a good look – White would have a "crusher" now, but can you find it? Simply 20. ♕g3!, threatening both 21. ♕xc7 and 21. ♗g6 wins, for if 20...♚d8 21. ♕xc7+! ♚xc7 22. ♖xe7+ ♕xe7 23. ♖xe7+ ♚b8 is an easily winning endgame.

19. ...		♚f8
20. ♖xe7		♕xe7

21. ♖xe7	♚xe7
22. ♗c4!	♚d6
23. ♕g3+	1-0

On either king retreat, 24. ♕g7+ wins Black's bishop. Harry Golombek, the leading British chess writer at the time, called this game "a striking piece of chess magic." But I believe you can learn to occasionally play "magically" too, if only you'll put in the work.

6. Göring Gambit Declined
Jay Whitehead – Peter Biyiasas
Lone Pine 1977

1. e4	e5
2. ♘f3	♘c6
3. d4	exd4
4. c3	…

This is the Göring Gambit. White sacrifices a pawn for increased center control and a small lead in development. Many strong players accept the second pawn because they believe White's compensation is insufficient, and they have studied the ensuing complications. But *you* haven't! Therefore, I suggest you decline the gambit as GM Biyiasas does here.

4. ...   d3

By returning the "booty" you deprive White's king bishop and queen knight of their ideal squares (c4 and c3 respectively), while buying time to effectively develop your own pieces. This simple way of handling the Göring Gambit was also recommended by the great Estonian GM, Paul Keres.

5. ♗xd3   ♗c5

While the cautious 5...d6 is often seen, this aggressive bishop move is quite playable.

6. 0-0	**d6**
7. b4	**♗b6**
8. a4	**...**

What is White threatening? What is Black's best response?

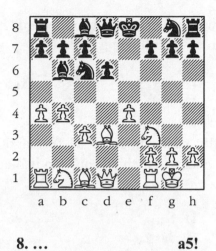

8. ...   **a5!**

White wanted to trap the bishop with 9. a5. Curiously, several books recommend 8...a6, including the amateur's "bible," *Modern Chess Openings,* 14th edition, which even claims White is slightly better after 9. ♘a3 (intending 10. ♘c4). However, 8...a5! is more *forcing* – you only should have already decided where to put the knight after White's obvious next move.

9. b5   **...**

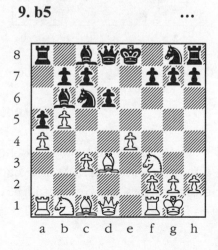

9. ...   ♘e5

Why go backward when you can go forward? Indeed, Black has nothing to fear from the following trade.

10. ♘xe5   dxe5
11. ♗a3   ...

While normally controlling the a3-f8 diagonal *before* Black has castled is advantageous, this is only so if Black intends to "go kingside"!

11. ...   ♗e6
12. ♕e2   ...

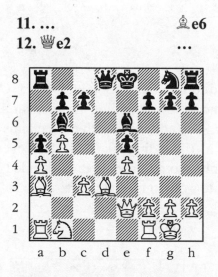

So, how would you bring out your pieces here?

12. ...   ♕h4!

Planning on 13...♘f6, followed by a timely hop to either g4 or f4 (via h5) with a tremendous attack. White starts playing badly here, not appreciating the danger. He should have developed his remaining knight to f3, via d2, ASAP!

13. ♔h1?	♞f6
14. g3	...

Apparently, only now does White realize that 14. f3? would allow 14...♞h5!, threatening 15...♞g3#! Notice it is Black's dark-squared bishop which really controls a crucial diagonal, and that it is now Black who is better developed.

14. ...	♛h3
15. f3	0-0-0
16. ♗c2	...

Played so the bishop won't be "hanging" after White's planned 17. ♛g2, but Black's next move prevents this (and would be equally strong had White played 16. ♗e7). As White's king has no escape squares, can you threaten mate?

16. ...	♞h5!
17. ♖g1	♖d7!

Yes, 17...♗xg1 wins the exchange, but a really good player knows when to apply Emanuel Lasker's dictum: "if you see a good move, don't play it at once, first look for a better one." Here, sim-

ply doubling rooks on the d-file will win faster as White is completely helpless.

18. ♖g2   ♖hd8
19. ♗c1   ...

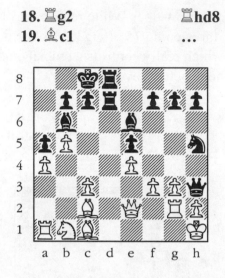

Probably played in a desperate attempt to bring his knight out
(to d2), but it is too late! White is playing without his queen knight
and rook while, as in the previous game, the winner is using *all* his
major and minor pieces. Now can you find a clever pair of *deflec-
tions* to finish White off?

19. ...   ♗c4!

The bishop may not be captured, due to 20...♖d1+ with a quick
checkmate.

20. ♕e1   ...

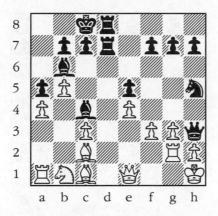

White's only playable move but it allows a stunning follow-up. Do you see it?

20. ...   ♗**f1!**

0-1

If White plays 21. ♕xf1, as the rook has no safe squares, then 21...♘xg3+ forces mate in three. An entertaining example of what can happen when you use *all* of your pieces and your opponent doesn't!

7. Alekhine's Defense
Ilya Gurevich – K.K. Karanja
New York 1987
U.S. Cadet Championship (under 16)

1. e4   ♘**f6**

(see diagram next page)

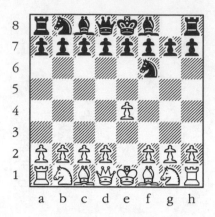

Alekhine's Defense is a controversial attempt to provoke White into building a large pawn center that Black will then try to destroy by sniping away at it! Still 2. e5, gaining *space,* is White's only serious way of seeking a sustained advantage against this opening.

2. e5	♘**d5**
3. d4	**d6**
4. ♘f3	**g6**

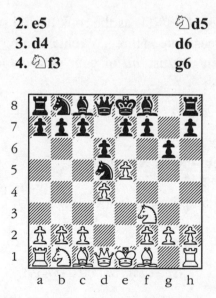

White is playing the Modern Variation. Nowadays, White is usually content with securing a modest space advantage, rather than hurling his c- and f-pawns forward on moves three and four, trying to blow Black off the board quickly.

| 5. ♗c4 | ♘b6 |
| 6. ♗b3 | ♗g7 |

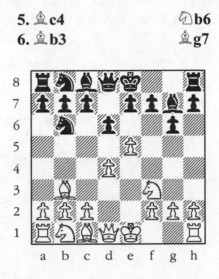

Already reaching a critical position in this opening. White must decide how to deal with Black's "threat" of 7...dxe5, with a possible queen trade afterwards, while not losing control of the e5 square (by playing 7. dxe5). A major, and quite controversial, variation here is 7. a4 dxe5 8. a5 ♘6d7 9. ♗xf7+!? ♔xf7 10. ♘g5+ ♔g8 with great complications. Gurevich's move is simpler and leads to a small but lasting advantage.

7. ♕e2	d5
8. 0-0	0-0
9. h3!	...

Preventing 9...♗g4, with the idea of trading off one of White's potential kingside attackers. This suggests Black should have played 8...♗g4! instead of castling, while White should have reversed his move order with 8. h3!.

39

9. ...	♘a6

An odd-looking move, but clearly Black wants to play ...c7-c5 soon, chipping away at White's strong center.

10. a4!	...

White wants to discourage Black from 10...c5 while also seizing space on the queenside – and succeeds! Perhaps Black feared variations like 10...c5 11. a5 ♘d7? 12. ♗xd5 ♘xe5 13. ♗xb7! ♗xb7 14. dxe5 ♗xf3 15. ♕xf3 ♗xe5? 16. ♕e2! when he drops a piece. However, after 11. a5, 11...c4! works out to be OK for Black, so White should probably just reinforce his strong center with 12. c3. Still, this is better than what happens after...

10. ...	♗e6?
11. a5	♘d7

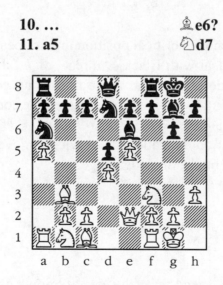

Now White has a simple move that irretrievably damages Black's pawn structure while, in effect, "cutting the board in two," with most of Black's men being on the wrong side! What is it?

12. ♘g5!   ...

Black cannot move the bishop because the d5-pawn would be hanging.

12. ...	c5
13. ♘xe6	fxe6
14. c3	♘c7
15. ♗e3	...

White is developing *all* of his pieces before beginning the final assault. Black now attempts to generate some counterplay on the queenside, but his position is too cramped for this to work.

15. ...	b6
16. axb6	axb6
17. ♘d2	...

Black is in a quandary. If he trades rooks, White gets the only open file. Probably, he should play 17...♖f7 followed by 18... ♘f8, hunker down, and pray! His next move releases the central tension in an attempt to continue aggression on the queenside, but it drives the bishop where it wants to go.

17. …	c4?
18. ♗c2	b5
19. ♘f3	♘b6
20. ♘g5	♕d7?

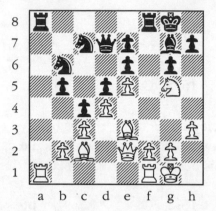

Black overlooks the threat, but after 20…♖f5 (forced) 21. g4!, followed by f2-f4, Black has a very bad position. So, how did White punish a king that's attacked by four pieces but defended by only two?

21. ♘xh7!	♔xh7
22. ♕h5+	♔g8
23. ♗xg6!	…

The most accurate capture because after…

| 23. … | ♖f5 |
| 24. ♕h7+ | ♔f8 |

…White can win immediately. How?

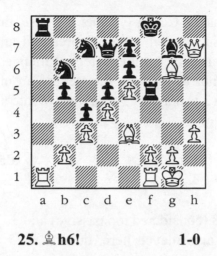

25. ♗h6!   **1-0**

For if 25…♗xh6, 26. ♕h8#. It is tragicomic how detached Black's queen and minor pieces are from their king's defense.

8. *Scandinavian Defense*
I.A. Horowitz – F. Kibberman
Warsaw Chess Olympiad 1935

1. e4   **d5**

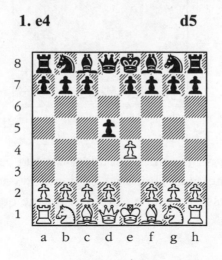

Also known as the Center Counter Defense, this sharp, aggressive reply by Black often makes unprepared amateurs both annoyed and anxious. Black immediately challenges White's control of d5 and e4 – not to mention threatening an unprotected pawn – so, while 2. ♘c3 is playable, what must White's next move be to keep the initiative?

| 2. exd5 | ♕xd5 |
| 3. ♘c3 | ♕a5 |

Both 3...♕d8 (considered too passive) and 3...♕d6 (the "hot" new move) are also played here, but 3...♕a5 is still probably Black's best, although his "active" queen will soon have to retreat with a consequent loss of time.

| 4. d4 | ♘f6 |
| 5. ♘f3 | ♗g4 |

Today this move is somewhat under a cloud because of the aggressive, resolute plan Horowitz begins now, and either 5...c6 (creating a necessary avenue of retreat for the queen) or 5...♗f5 are preferred.

6. h3	♗h5
7. g4!	♗g6
8. ♘e5	...

I first learned of this game from my friend and fellow chess teacher, Peter J. Tamburro, Jr., who used it in a video lecture in his terrific series entitled *Chess Openings for Amateurs,* which ran on the Internet radio station/website ICC Chess.FM in 2008. Pete pointed out that while "We teach young players to avoid moving the kingside pawns, especially if your opponent hasn't castled on that side, White's compensation here is reasonable. He gets a nicely posted knight which not only attacks f7 and d7, but may also move to c4 to harass the black queen."

8. ...	c6(?)

Not strictly necessary yet, as both *MCO* and *NCO* give 8...e6 9. ♗g2 c6 10. h4 ♗e4 11. ♗xe4 ♘xe4 12. ♕f3 ♘d6 13. ♗f4 f6 14. ♘d3 as the main line, with White having a definite advantage. Apparently after 8...e6, Horowitz's 9. ♘c4 is not so strong because Black can play 9...♕a6! as White has no winning *discovery* with the c4-knight and 10. ♗f4, threatening 11. ♘d6+, is met by 11...♕c6! when Black looks to be OK.

9. ♘c4!	♕c7?

Now, of course, 9...♕a6?? is no good (10. ♘d6+!), but Horowitz's next move suggests that this, too, is inaccurate and 9...♕d8 would have been better. Although c7 is the normal retreat square for Black's queen in this opening, it is a mistake in this position. Can you find a surprising developing move that not only intends further harassment of Black's queen, but at the same time sets an insidious trap?

10. ♕f3!!   **♗xc2?**

Black takes the bait. Relatively best was 10...e6 11. ♗f4 ♕d8 12. 0-0-0 with an awful position. But after...

11. ♗f4   **♕d8**

...what did White play?

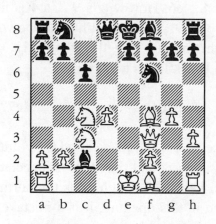

12. ♕e2!   **...**

Backwards queen moves that attack along new ranks, diagonals and/or files are particularly hard to spot. This *double threat*, attacking the bishop while simultaneously pinning the e7-pawn, is a killer. Now Black's king will be forced to go for a walk.

12. ...	♗g6
13. ♘d6+	♔d7
14. ♘xb7	♕b6
15. ♘c5+	♔c8

Take a good look at Black's miserable position below. This is exactly what you are trying to avoid in the opening! But material is even and the game still has to be won, so what did White do?

| 16. ♗g2 | e6 |
| 17. 0-0 | ... |

He simply brought out his last minor piece and castled, secure in the knowledge that Black's "shaky" king and retarded development should not survive a coordinated attack by *all* of White's pieces. Black's next move, seeking relief through exchanges, only makes things worse because the c-file is opened – but it is hard to give Black good advice here.

17. ...	♘d5?
18. ♘xd5	cxd5
19. ♖ac1	♚d8
20. ♗g5+!	♗e7
21. ♗xe7+	♚xe7
22. ♗xd5	...

While Black's position is pretty sad, why didn't he at least try 22...♘c6, which appears to save the exchange?

Since 22...♘c6 allows the winning sacrifice 23. ♘xe6!, he played instead...

22. ...	♘d7
23. ♗xa8	♖xa8
24. ♘xd7	♚xd7
25. ♖fd1	♛b7
26. d5	exd5
27. ♛e5!	1-0

The *coup de grâce*. A model attacking game against an uncastled king.

9. Réti's Opening
B. Andonov – W. Watson
St. John (2nd International) 1988

1. ♘f3	d5
2. c4	d4

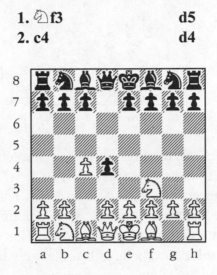

Black plays the most aggressive move, seizing space and attacking important squares in White's camp. The game evolves into a kind of Reversed Benoni, although I believe White's extra tempo still leads to no more than equality against correct play.

3. g3	♘c6

While 3...c5 is often played here to reinforce Black's control of d4, Watson prefers speedy development of his minor pieces.

4. ♗g2	e5
5. d3	♗b4+(!)

This curious check requires some explanation. First of all, 6. ♗d2 would surely have been met by 6…a5, which restricts any possible future queenside expansion by White and Black is ready, if 7. ♗xb4, to recapture with the a-pawn, creating a useful semi-open file. If White instead plays 7. a3 then Black trades bishops himself, having at least exchanged his relatively bad bishop – that is, the one blocked by its own center pawns.

6. ♘bd2	**a5!**

This move is still necessary, as otherwise White plays 7. a3, forcing Black either to trade his bishop for a knight, or to retreat with loss of time while White expands on the queenside for free with 8. b4. Possibly another idea Watson had in mind with 5… ♗b4+ is that after 6. ♘bd2 White can no longer maneuver this knight to c2 (via a3), where it would support a thematic queenside pawn advance.

7. 0-0	**♘f6**
8. ♘e1?	**…**

The beginning of a bad plan. 8. a3 ♗c5 (or 8…♗e7) 9. ♖b1 was more consistent with White's strategy in this type of position.

8. ...	0-0
9. e4	...

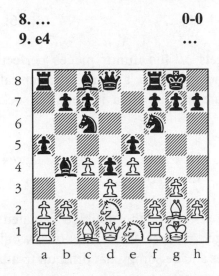

I have deliberately given no annotation to this move! Good, bad or indifferent? And how should Black respond?

9. ...	dxe3 e.p.!

Really, this reply to White's mistaken idea should be automatic, and, frankly, it would be for an expert/master strength player, but I will give you credit not only for remembering that the *en passant* capture is possible (!), but for evaluating the resulting positions correctly whether you make it or not. Clearly, you don't want to allow White to "get away" with blocking the center in this way, so that *he* will get attacking chances on the kingside by moves such as 10. h3 and 11. f4. *Remember that opening up a position almost always favors the better-developed side.*

10. fxe3	♗g4
11. ♕c2	...

Now what? Perhaps one of your minor pieces needs to be repositioned?

11. ...   ♗c5!

Yes! Black gets *all* his minor pieces perfectly placed while gaining time attacking White's vulnerable central pawn mass. As White's pieces are in a bit of a jumble, he seeks relief through exchanges.

12. ♘e4   ♘xe4
13. ♗xe4   ...

Oddly, 13. dxe4!?, allowing doubled, isolated e-pawns, might have lasted longer as these "ugly" fellows would control many important squares and be somewhat difficult to attack. However, it is hard to accept voluntarily such weaknesses during actual play! Watson now commences a standard attacking scheme. How?

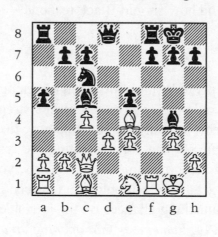

13. ...   f5!

Intending to use the f-pawn as a battering ram against the *pinned* pawn on e3, and also g3 which shields White's king. While White's next move seems to gain a tempo, he loses it right back again with the forced 15. a3, which is needed to prevent 15...♘b4 forking the queen and bishop.

14. ♗d5+	♔h8
15. a3	f4
16. ♘g2	♛g5!

The *long, strong queen move* again, this time further pressuring e3 and White's kingside. White's next two moves attempt to break the pin on e3, but after…

17. gxf4	exf4
18. d4	…

…how did Black cross him up?

18. …	**f3!**

If the knight moves, then 19…♗f5+ wins the queen, so White is forced into the following exchanges.

19. dxc5	fxg2
20. ♖xf8+	♖xf8
21. ♛xg2??	…

But now 20. ♗xg2 was forced, although after 20…♘e5 Black has a ferocious attack and White is still playing without his

53

remaining two queenside pieces. What astonishing dénouement did Watson now have planned, or perhaps discover?

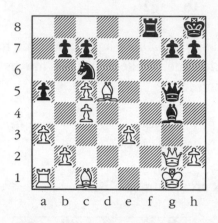

21. ...   ♗h3!!

Of course, now "resigns" would be White's correct move, 22. ♕xg5 being met by 22...♖f1#, but "hope springs eternal" so...

22. e4?!?   ♕xg2#

An efficient, perfect attacking game in which GM Watson did not waste a single move and, of course, used *all* of his pieces.

10. Queen's Pawn, Barry Attack
Luis Palau – Jan-Willem te Kolsté
London Chess Olympiad 1927

1. ♘f3	♘f6
2. d4	g6
3. ♘c3	d5(!)

If White doesn't have the guts to put his e-pawn on e4 on move one, don't let him do it "for free" on move four! Unless you really want to play a Pirc or Modern Defense, 3...d5 is the only correct move here.

4. ♗f4 ...

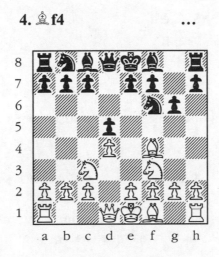

Now known as the Barry Attack, this system of simple development against fianchetto defenses was briefly popular during the 1920's, and was even used by Capablanca. It resurfaced in the early 1980's, at first introduced into British tournaments by GM Niaz Murshed from Bangladesh, and later consistently adopted by GM Mark Hebden, one of the top English players. Curiously, "Barry" is British slang for rubbish, although if White is allowed to carry out his simple plan of castling queenside and attacking quickly by pushing his h-pawn, it can be quite dangerous. But what if Black goes after the bishop right away?

4. ... ♘h5(?)

Probably a waste of time as Black, to get the bishop, will have to slightly compromise his pawn structure and give White a useful semi-open file. Nowadays Black usually reacts against the Barry with aggression in the center by 4...♗g7 5. e3 0-0 6. ♗e2 c5! 7. ♘e5 ♘c6 8. 0-0 cxd4 9. exd4 ♕b6 10. ♘xc6 ♕xc6 11. ♖e1 a6 with equal chances, as in Mark Hebden – Robert Ruck, Calvià Olympiad 2004.

5. ♗e5!	f6
6. ♗g3	♘xg3
7. hxg3	♗g7
8. e3	...

Yes, 8. e4!? is also possible but it also opens up the game for Black's bishops.

8. ...	c6

Not in itself a bad move, but preparing a big mistake! 8...♗e6, with the idea of 9...♗f7, was much safer.

9. ♗d3	e5?

Black is completely oblivious to his vulnerability along the h5-e8 diagonal, probably thinking that his attack in the center and attendant threats (10...e4) were paramount. What move did he overlook... *and how far do you have to calculate before playing it?*

10. ♖xh7!	♔f7

This is probably Black's best chance, as 10...e4 is bad because of 11. ♖xg7 exd3 12. ♕xd3! and 10...♖xh7 11. ♗xg6+ is simply hopeless. So you only had to calculate a couple of moves to play 10. ♖xh7!, but having gotten this far, now take another good, long look at the position in front of you before deciding if being a pawn ahead is the best you can do. Can Black's king's shelter be blown away?

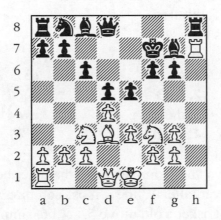

11. ♗xg6+!!	♔xg6
12. ♘xe5+!	...

You had to *see* not just this second sacrifice to make the first, but also the follow-up – our old friend the long, strong queen move! Of course, if 12...♔f5(g5), then 13. ♕g4 is mate!

12. ...	fxe5
13. ♕h5+	♔f6
14. ♕xe5+	♔f7

If 14...♔g6 15. ♕xg7+ ♔f5 16. g4+! ♔e6 17. ♕e5#.

15. ♕xg7+	♔e6
16. ♕e5#	

An impressive miniature which demonstrates that, while you often don't have to see very far ahead to make a combination gaining the advantage, once you get there you should take another long, hard look – you never know what extra "goodies" you may find!

11. Scotch Game, Mieses Variation
"Lena" – P. Tamburro
Internet Chess Club 2009

1. e4		e5	
2. ♘f3		♘c6	
3. d4		exd4	
4. ♘xd4		♘f6	

One of the two "best" moves here, the other being my favorite 4...♝c5. However, after White's most common reply, 5. ♝e3, I prefer Emanuel Lasker's old move 5...♝b6, simply protecting the bishop, rather than the popular, heavily analyzed 5...♛f6.

5. ♘xc6		bxc6	
6. e5!?		...	

This very aggressive continuation was resuscitated by then-World Champion Gary Kasparov against Anatoly Karpov and others, after he discovered that the standard evaluation of easy equality for Black in the goofy-looking position after 6...♕e7 7. ♕e2 ♘d5 8. c4 ♗a6 was not entirely accurate. Soon, reams of opening theory evolved from this position, so it is not surprising that the tireless chess teacher, author, and researcher, Pete Tamburro, who – like myself – tries to avoid "trendy" lines when possible, sought another path for Black.

6. ...   ♘e4!?

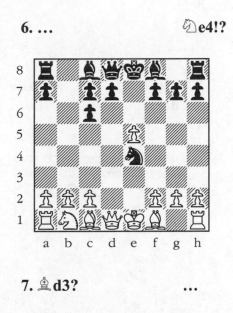

7. ♗d3?   ...

Confronted by an unusual response, White immediately goes wrong. Now he will either lose back the tempo or have to give up the *bishop pair*. If you ever try this line yourself, you should be aware of White's two major alternatives:

a. 7. ♕d4?!, which is frowned upon because of 7...f5! 8. f3 ♗c5 9. ♕c4 d5! 10. ♕a4 0-0! 11. ♕xc6 ♕h4+ 12. g3 ♘xg3 13. hxg3 ♕xg3+ 14. ♔d2 ♕xf3 15. ♕xc5 ♕xh1 15. ♕f2 with a wild and woolly position favoring Black, which he eventually won (J.

Lautier – A. Beliavsky, Biel 1992). (Incidentally, Pete himself won a fun "quickie" recently after 9. ♕a4? ♕h4+ 10. g3 ♕h5!11. fxe4 ♕f3 12. ♕c4 ♗f2+! 13. ♔d2 ♕e3+ 14. ♔d1 ♕e1#.)

b. 7. ♗e3 d5 8. exd6 cxd6 9. ♗d3 ♘f6 10. 0-0 ♗e7 11. c4 0-0 12. ♘c3 13. ♖e1 ♗e6, which is supposed to be slightly better for White although Korchnoi drew it in 37 moves (J. Timman – V. Korchnoi, Sarajevo 1984). I certainly think Black's position is viable and most of you won't have to defend it against a *super-grandmaster* too often!

7. ...	♘c5
8. ♗c4	d5
9. exd6	cxd6
10. 0-0	d5
11. ♖e1+	...

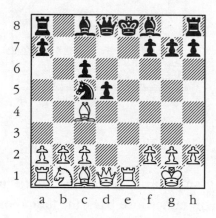

What's the best way to block the check?

11. ...	♗e6!

Certainly not the passive 11...♗e7, as this bishop should be pointed at h2. Pete has big plans for this piece!

12. ♗e2	♗d6
13. ♗g4	0-0
14. ♗xe6	♘xe6
15. ♘c3(?)	...

This is really an example of "mindless development" as the knight would serve White much better defensively on f3 (via 15. ♘d2). Still, Black would stand significantly better as he controls the entire center and has more aggressively posted pieces. Now if you were an experienced competitor like Pete, would you play the obvious threat (15...♕h4) or bring another potential attacker into position first?

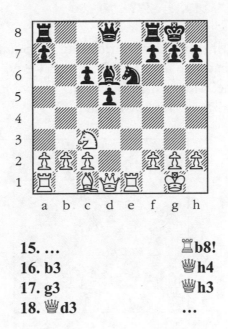

15. ...	♖b8!
16. b3	♕h4
17. g3	♕h3
18. ♕d3	...

Can Black bring another piece into the attack?

18. ...	♖b4!
19. ♘e2??	...

This is a terrible blunder overlooking the point behind Black's last move. He had to play 19. ♕f1, which we will examine at the end of the game. Meanwhile, how can you *point almost all your pieces at White's king* and finish him off?

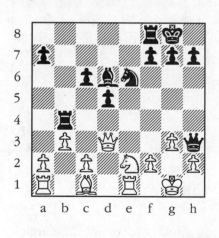

19. ...	♖h4!
20. gxh4	♗xh2+
21. ♔h1	♗g3+(!)

Even if Black's queen were not *en prise,* this discovery check is almost always the correct one in this type of combination. Remember you must also attack f2 twice, as it is usually the mating square.

22. ♔g1   ♛h2+
0-1

Now let's look at the position after White's best chance, 19. ♛f1, which is what Pete expected. What would you do?

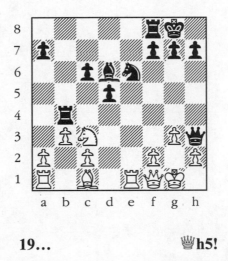

19...   ♛h5!

Pete commented to me in an email that, "...intuitively 19... ♛h5 would have been my choice... too many holes around the king to simplify." He then gave a sample continuation:

20. ♗a3   ♞g5
21. ♗xb4   ♗xb4
22. ♛e2   ...

If 22. ♛d3, then 22...♛f3! wins, as 22. ♛xf3 ♞xf3+ loses a piece, and either 23. ♛ or ♖e2 (to prevent mate on f2) allows 23...♞h3+ 24. ♔f1 ♛h1#.

| 22. ... | ♕xe2 |
| 23. ♖xe2 | ♗xc3 |

With two minor pieces for a rook, which is a winning endgame (though still requiring some hard work).

GRECO'S SACRIFICE,
OR THE GREEK GIFT

This classical bishop sacrifice, occurring on either h7 or h2, is the most important standard attacking combination against a castled king you will have to learn. It was discovered by Gioachino Greco, perhaps the first professional chess master, early in the seventeenth century, and first appears as a complete game or analysis in his famous book *Le Jeu des Eschets*, Paris, 1669.

Below is a casual game played by my friend and colleague, Bruce Alberston, against an amateur in 1986, in which Bruce reaches a very similar position at move 11 (see next diagram) to the one given by Greco in his book nearly 300 years ago! The opening is a c3 Sicilian, an unusually logical name for an opening, as it merely indicates that White meets the Sicilian Defense, 1. e4 c5, with the move 2. c3.

12. Sicilian Defense, c3 Variation
Bruce Alberston – amateur
New York (casual game) 1986

1. e4 c5 2. c3 ♘f6 3. e5 ♘d5 4. d4 cxd4 5.cxd4 e6 6. ♘f3 ♘c6 7. ♘c3 ♘xc3 8. bxc3 ♗e7 9. ♗d3 0-0? ((9…d6 is better) **10. h4!** (this should have set off warning signals in Black's mind, but…) **10…d6??** (if 10…h6, Bruce intended the powerful *rook lift* 11. ♖h3!, with a strong attack, but now it is all over. Why?):

11. ♗xh7+! ♔xh7 12. ♘g5+ ♗xg5 (on 12...♔g8, 13. ♕h5 leads to a quick mate, while 12...♔g6 13. h5+ will win the queen or the king!) **13. hxg5+ ♔g6** (or 13...♔g8 14. ♕h5 f6 15. g6, and Black is *kaput*) **14. ♕h5+ ♔f5 15. ♕h3+ 1-0**

For if 15...♔g6, then 16. ♕h7#.

Now for another typical, and perhaps even more fundamental, example of *Greco's Sacrifice*, where the preliminary move h2-h4, further reinforcing White's control of the g5 square, is not required. This game, played by GM Michael Rohde in the "4 Rated Games Thursday Night" tournament at New York City's Marshall Chess Club in September 2008, is not only quite instructive, but could have had an unusual "twist" near the end! The opening is another c3 Sicilian, and Mike's opponent was then an A-class player, i.e., a strong amateur with a U.S. Chess Federation rating of approximately 1800.

13. Sicilian Defense, c3 Variation
Michael Rohde – amateur
New York, Marshall Chess Club 2008

1. e4 c5 2. c3 ♘f6 3. e5 ♘d5 4. d4 cxd4 5. ♘f3 (a useful finesse, because some people just don't look!) **5...e6 6. cxd4 d6 7. a3** (a useful move, first discovered by Rohde over twenty years ago, which takes away the b4 square from Black's pieces) **7... dxe5 8. dxe5 ♗c5?** (8...♗e7 is correct as this piece is needed to guard squares on the kingside) **9. ♗d3 0-0??** (What now? Do you see the pattern?):

10. ♗xh7+! ♔xh7 11. ♘g5+ ♔g8 (11...♔g6 12. h4! with a quick finish – see the next two games) **12. ♕h5** (But here comes the "twist." Black blundered with 12...♖e8??, but how could he have prolonged the game?):

With 12...♘f6! 13. exf6 ♛d3!, protecting h7, Black is still breathing, though after 14. fxg7 ♚xg7 15. ♘c3 ♛g6 16. ♛e2 he is a pawn down in a bad position.

But after 12...♜e8??, the end comes swiftly with 13. ♛xf7+! ♚h8 14. ♛h5+ ♚g8 15. ♛h7+ ♚f8 16. ♛h8+ ♚e7 17. ♛xg7#. Note that 13. ♛h7+? would allow Black's king to escape via e7. When you think you can finish someone off, take it slow!

(Incidentally, I have given the last two games in paragraphed rather than columnar notation, not only because the annotations are less elaborate than most of the other games in this book, but also to begin to get you used to playing over recorded games in this popular, space-saving format. Much of the material you may need to study to further progress is published in this format.) The next two games, played by the author almost exactly thirty years apart, are remarkable because the nearly identical combinative finishes which occurred evolved from two very different openings! Additionally, the strategy of taking over the center and driving off the primary defender – the f6-(f3-)knight – was the same. Vanity aside, I think you will find them quite instructive.

14. Sicilian Defense, Löwenthal Variation
Frank Kuhnrich – Fred Wilson
New York (casual game) 1966

1. e4	c5
2. ♘f3	♘c6
3. d4	cxd4
4. ♘xd4	e5?!

Nowadays I often play this risky and provocative line against new post-beginner or intermediate adult students to gauge how they react to the myriad choices this move forces upon them. It is interesting that almost no one discovers – or, more correctly, *works out* – the strongest reply, when first confronted with 4...e5 in this position. What do you think it is?

5. ♘xc6?   ...

Certainly not this, although it was once actually played by Morphy! While playable, this move is exactly what Black wants! Not only is his pawn majority in the center strengthened, but also Black's potential to assume significantly superior central control has increased.

In fact, White has five other knight moves to consider, though two of them, 5. ♘e2 (too passive) and 5. ♘f5? (which allows 5...d5! with an edge for Black), are clearly wrong. And while 5. ♘b3 or 5. ♘f3 are OK, they tend to transpose back into acceptable Sicilian variations where Black's hole (weak square) at d5 is compensated for by his control of d4 and his backward d-pawn can be adequately defended. So an experienced modern player would almost certainly play 5. ♘b5! here, not only threatening 6. ♘d6+ gaining the advantage of the two bishops, but, after 5...d6, making the hole at d5 permanent with 6. c4! which current opening theory considers to give White a small edge leading into the middlegame.

5. ...	bxc6
6. ♗d3	...

Developing the bishop more actively by 6. ♗c4 is better, and most often played here, but the text move does set a trap. Can't Black simply play 6...d5 now?

No! For if 6...d5?, then 7. exd5 cxd5 8. ♗b5+! forces either 8...♚e7 putting Black's king in jeopardy, or 8...♗d7 9. ♛xd5, winning a pawn. I actually came up with an interesting, spur-of-the-moment gambit here which I got to repeat in a serious practice game against an adult student nearly three decades later, and many more times in five-minute games since then.

6. ...	f5!?
7. exf5	...

This is *forced;* however, in a training game played in 1995, White played the insufficiently thought-out 7. f4?, when after 7...fxe4 8. ♗xe4 ♘f6 9. ♗d3 e4! 10. ♗e2 ♗c5 White already had a horrible position.

7. ...	♘f6
8. 0-0?!	...

The best move is 8. g4! turning the game into a strange kind of "reversed" King's Gambit Accepted. However, after 8...h6 (forced) Black obviously has good compensation for the pawn (a big, strong center after 9...d5).

8. ...	d5
9. ♖e1	♗d6
10. c4	...

Desperately trying to chip away at Black's powerful center.

10. ...	0-0
11. ♘c3	e4
12. ♗f1	...

Does Black have to defend d5 further?

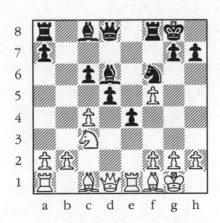

12. ...	♗xf5!
13. cxd5	cxd5
14. ♘xd5??	...

71

The losing blunder, though after 14. g3 or 14. h3 White's position is not enviable. He clearly thought I overlooked that after 14...♘xd5, 15. ♕xd5+ is check! But let's see: Black has a bishop pointing at h2 (defended only by the king), a knight that can safely go to g4 and a queen to h4, hmmm…

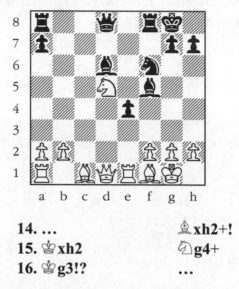

14. …	♗xh2+!
15. ♔xh2	♘g4+
16. ♔g3!?	…

16. ♔g1 loses to 16...♕h4 17. ♗f4 ♕xf2+ 18. ♔h1 ♗e6! (threatening 19...♖xf4! with mate or serious material loss to follow). As 16...♕d6+? allows White some respite after 17. ♗f4, what new unit must you now add to your attacking force?

16. ...	**h5!**

There is no answer to this.

17. ♗c4	**h4+**
18. ♔f4	**...**

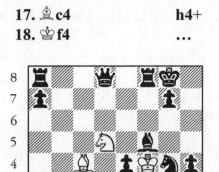

18. ...	♛d6+
19. ♔g5	♛h6#

Checkmate. But return to the last diagram for a moment. Did you, like myself and many others (except my colleague Emmitt Jefferson) overlook 18...g5(!) mate? It is odd to see a queen defending a checkmating pawn rather than the other way around!

15. Queen's Gambit Declined, Semi-Slav Defense
Fred Wilson – Oshon Temple
New York (5-minute game) 1996

1. d4	♘f6
2. ♘f3	**d5**
3. c4	**c6**

4. ♘c3   **e6**

In the Slav Defense proper, Black plays 4...dxc4 here, pretty much forcing the response 5. a4, unless White wants to play a gambit by allowing Black to defend the c-pawn with 5...b5.

5. e3   **♗b4**

A much more standard developing scheme for Black here is 5...♘bd7 followed by 6...♗d6.

6. ♗d3   **dxc4**
7. ♗xc4   **♘e4?**

Does White really have to defend c3?

8. 0-0!   **♗xc3**

Not 8...♘xc3 9. bxc3 ♗xc3 10. ♖b1 0-0 (otherwise 11. ♗a3!) 11. ♕c2 ♗a5 12. e4, with a strong center and the initiative in return for the pawn.

9. bxc3   **0-0(?)**

Now Black should probably follow the maxim "in for a penny, in for a pound" and play 9...♘xc3 10. ♕c2 ♘d5 11. e4 ♘e7 (or 11...♘b6), though here too White obviously has great compensation for the pawn with his advantage in development and center control.

10. ♗d3!	**♘f6**

But now 10. ♘xc3 fails to 11. ♕c2!.

11. e4	**c5**

As in the previous game, hoping to chip away at my strong center. Anyone who would play 12. dxc5? here should please leave the room!

12. e5	**♘fd7**

You know what to do now, right?

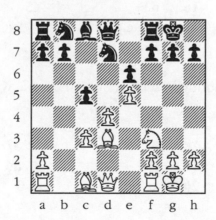

13. ♗xh7+!	**♚xh7**
14. ♘g5+	**♚g6**

What is White's most accurate continuation?

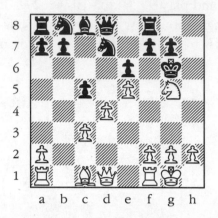

15. h4!	...

As 15. ♕g4 f5 16. exf6 ♘xf6 is messy, this move, threatening simply 16. h5+, is best. The rest is easy.

15. ...	♖h8
16. ♕d3+	f5
17. exf6+ e.p.	♔xf6
18. ♕f3+	...

The point of luring Black's rook to the h-file where it no longer defends f7.

18. ...	♔e7
19. ♕f7+	♔d6
20. ♕xe6+	1-0

ATTACKING
A FIANCHETTO CASTLED POSITION

Perhaps Bobby Fischer put it best. When discussing how he demolished GM Bent Larsen's Sicilian Dragon at Portorož 1958, after the players had castled on opposite sides, he wrote, "I'd won dozens of skittles games in analogous positions and had it down to a science: pry open the h-file, sac, sac... mate!" *(My 60 Memorable Games,* New York, 1969). To which I would add that you usually want to trade off your opponent's fianchettoed bishop by making a *battery* with your queen and bishop on the c1-h6 diagonal when playing White and, of course, reversing this setup to the c8-h3 diagonal if you have Black.

In five of the six games that follow, you will see how easy it is to carry out Bobby's "simple attacking plan" with the white pieces against unwary or inexperienced players. And in our sixth example the great world title contender, GM Victor Korchnoi, develops a devastating attack with Black out of a fairly tranquil opening, also against Bent Larsen!

16. Pirc/Modern Defense
O. Temple – Andrews
New York 1996

1. ♘c3	♘f6
2. e4	d6
3. d4	g6

Although Oshon transposes into a Pirc or Modern Defense from Van Geet's Opening (1. ♘c3!?), you can obviously also reach it via 1. e4 or 1. d4. The Pirc Defense, named after the Yugoslav GM Vasja Pirc who played and promoted it during the decade immediately after World War II, was initially regarded with great suspicion by most grandmasters because Black cedes White almost total control of the center for the first 5-10 moves. Alekhine even referred to an early occurrence in 1924 as a "Joke Opening"! However, it is certainly a fighting defense, creating unbalanced, asymmetrical positions right from the start. And after its adoption by such solid, positionally oriented grandmasters as Mikhail Botvinnik and Yasser Seirawan, the Pirc had really arrived. While still rarely played by today's elite, the so-called "super-grandmasters," because of White's space advantage, it is very popular with the hoi polloi, i.e. most of *your opponents*.

3. ♗g5!   ...

While 4. f4, 4. f3 4. ♗e3 and 4. ♘f3 are played more frequently here, Oshon deserves an "exclam" for this move as he really thought up this dangerous *attacking pattern* over the board and implemented it very well! In fact, I was so impressed with this game and some of his subsequent victories in this variation that I adopted it myself, with great success. As it turns out, the "4. ♗g5 variation" has often been used by several top grandmasters, including currently Peter Lékó and Alexander Motylev, both of whom have won brilliant games with this line.

4. ...	**♗g7**
5. ♕d2	**0-0?**

John Nunn suggests Black should play 5...h6, followed by 6...g5!, forcing a trade for White's dark-squared bishop by either

7...♘h5 or 7...♘g4, depending on where White retreats it. Castling "into it" leads to trouble according to ECO.

6. 0-0-0	c6
7. h4	b5
8. f3	...

The position below, and ones like it, are exactly what Black should try to avoid when playing *fianchetto defenses*. He has no significant counterplay against the white king, and White's attack, via the consistent pawn moves g2-g4 and h2-h4-h5, along with ♗h6, is coming way too fast.

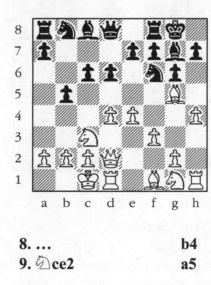

8. ...	b4
9. ♘ce2	a5

If Black had tried 9...♕a5, then 10. ♔b1 ♗e6 11. ♘c1, and Black's "attack" is over while White's is just beginning. Oshon told me he thought Black played 9...a5 to protect the b4-pawn, which he (and, I hope, you also!) had absolutely no intention of taking!

10. g4	♗a6

11. ♔b1 ...

While often a useful prophylactic move, this is not strictly necessary here, as Black's counterplay is developing much too slowly.

11. ... ♘bd7
12. h5 ♗xe2?

Here 12...♖e8 had to be played, though White has a winning attack already. By the way, how should White recapture?

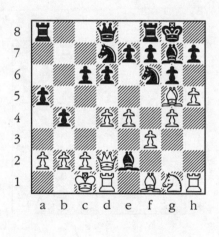

13. ♘xe2! ...

Because the knight can now quickly join in the attack and the f1-bishop will get its chance soon!

13. ... e5
14. ♗h6 c5
15. ♗xg7 ♔xg7
16. hxg6 fxg6
17. ♕h6+ ♔f7

If 17...♔g8, then 18. ♘g3 threatening g4-g5 and/or ♗c4+ is crushing.

18. g5	♘e8!?
19. ♕xh7+	♘g7

Black hopes to bail out into a lost ending by 20...♖h8 but he never gets the chance. What is White's most accurate continuation?

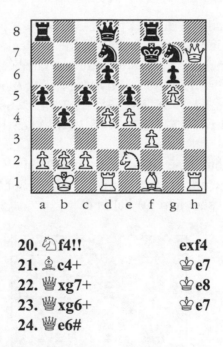

20. ♘f4!!	exf4
21. ♗c4+	♔e7
22. ♕xg7+	♔e8
23. ♕xg6+	♔e7
24. ♕e6#	

I append another similar, interesting game won by Oshon a year later, this time against Macauley Peterson who went on to create and star in the popular Internet chess video series *Chess Vibes*. It also demonstrates a useful tactical trick at the end, which Oshon found over the board but you should become familiar with now. (Note also the rating difference between the players. Oshon, who only began serious tournament play as a teenager and was one of my most talented students during the late 1990s, demonstrated again and again that a 200-300 rating point differential doesn't mean so much when neither player has reached the "expert" level of 2000.)

17. Pirc/Modern Defense
O. Temple (1483) – M. Peterson (1744)
NYC High School Championship 1997

1. ♘c3 d6 2. d4 g6 3. e4 ♝g7 4. f3 ♘f6 5. ♝g5 0-0(?) 6. ♕d2 ♖e8? (The beginning of a mistaken idea. Black thinks if he can preserve his fianchettoed bishop against a later ♝h6 by White, his king will be safer.) **7. 0-0-0 ♘bd7 8. g4 c5 9. ♘ge2 a6 10. h4 b5 11. h5 b4 12. ♘b1 ♕a5 13. a3! ♝b7 14. ♝h6 ♝h8 15. hxg6 hxg6 16. ♘g3 cxd4 17. ♕h2! ♕e5 18. f4 ♕c5 19. axb4 ♕xb4**

Black had thought he could slow down White's attack by avoiding the exchange of his dark-squared bishop, but White has a cool winning tactical shot here. What is it?

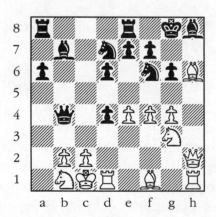

20. ♝f8! ♝g7?? (Obviously stunned by White's impossible-looking move 20, Black blunders badly. He had to play 20...♚xf8

21. ♕xh8+ ♘g8 22. ♖h7 ♖ec8 22. ♕g7+ ♔e8 23. ♕xf7+! ♔d8
24. ♕xg8+, when White has a winning position a full piece up.)
21. ♗xg7 ♔xg7 22. ♕h6+ 1-0

18. Pirc/Modern Defense
F. Wilson – Tabakman
New York 1997

1. ♘c3			♘f6
2. e4			d6
3. d4			g6
4. ♗g5!?			♗g7
5. ♕d2			...

Possibly 5. f3 is more accurate, as Black could now force a trade of his f6-knight for White's dark-squared bishop by 5...h6 and 6...g5!, etc.

5. ...		0-0?
6. 0-0-0		...

Now White has a "ready-made" attacking position.

6. ...		♘c6
7. f3		♗d7
8. g4		♕c8?
9. ♗h6		e5
10. d5		♘d4

Giving Black one well-placed piece, which however is not enough to save a bad position. After swapping the bishops, what did White do?

11. ♗xg7		♔xg7

83

12. ♘ce2! ...

He simply traded it off!

12. ... ♘xe2
13. ♘xe2 ♗b5?

Black trades off White's worst piece! 13...h5! had to be tried, although 14. h4! inaugurates a ferocious attack (e.g., 14...hxg4 15. h5!, and if 15...gxh5 16. ♕g5+ wins a piece, or 15...♘xh5 16. ♖xh5! gxh5 17. ♕g5+ leads to mate).

14. ♘g3 ♗xf1
15. ♖dxf1 b5?
16. h4 ♕a6?

A "one-piece attack" rarely succeeds!

17. ♔b1 c5

What is the most accurate attacking move here? (Note that 20. h5 ♘g8 21. hxg6 fxg6 22. ♕h2 h6 will hold for a little while.)

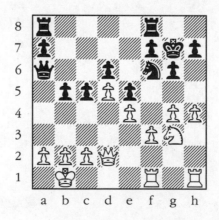

18. ♕g5!   ...

If 18...h6?, then 19. ♘f5+! wins easily.

18. ...   ♘g8
19. h5!   f6

Trying to push me back, hoping then to blockade the position by 20...g5. But how did White finish him off?

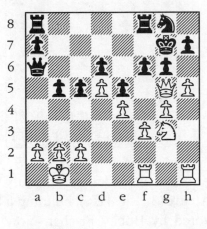

20. ♘f5+!   ♔f7

Forced, as 20...♔h8 allows 21. hxg6! fxg5 22. g7#! (or 22. ♖xh7#).

21. hxg6+   ♔e8
22. ♕h5   hxg6
23. ♕xg6+   ♔d8
24. ♕g7   ♖e8
25. ♖h7   1-0

19. Pirc/Modern Defense
Michael Adams – Peter Martin
London 2003

1. e4	g6
2. d4	♗g7
3. ♘c3	c6

This is a clever move order designed mainly to avoid the dangerous Austrian Attack (3...d6 4. f4), building a big, mobile pawn center, much favored by Bobby Fischer. Now 4. f4 d5!? 5. e5 (best) leads to a type of *closed position* called the Gurgenidze System that many players who love long, maneuvering games greatly enjoy. Hey, Petrosian even drew Fischer (!) with it in 1970. Also, my favorite line doesn't work here because on 4. ♗g5? Black has 4...♛b6!.

4. ♘f3	d6
5. ♗e3	♘f6
6. ♛d2	0-0?

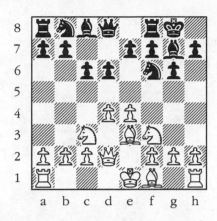

Again "castling into it," and again wrong! As IM Richard Palliser observed in his excellent annotations to this game in the June 2004 issue of the British magazine *Chess,* "…castling into the attack like this is really asking for it. Instead Black should aim to reduce the impact of (White's) ♗h6 with 6…b5, beginning immediate counterplay, or with 6…♕a5…" What follows is a fairly straightforward example of what happens when Black plays passively against this variation, which the English call the *150 Attack.*

7. ♗h6   ♘bd7
8. 0-0-0   b5

I'm sure Black would have liked to get in 8…e5? but it simply loses a pawn to 9. ♗xg7 ♔xg7 10. dxe5 dxe5 11. ♘xe5, and Black can't take the knight because of the *pin* on the d-file. *Remember, when you castle queenside to attack a fianchetto castled position you are usually creating not one, but two useful batteries* – the queen and bishop on the c1-h6 diagonal and the queen and rook on the d-file.

9. ♗xg7   ♔xg7

87

And now having eliminated one of Black's two vital defenders with your first *battery,* how can you use your other one to help drive off another guardian?

10. e5!	♞e8
11. h4!	...

Perhaps obvious to GM Adams but *you* still need to remember you must pry open the h-file.

11. ...	♞b6?

Probably 11...h5 is necessary (as in the previous game), though after either 12. ♗d3 or 12. ♞g5 White has a substantial advantage in space and a strong attack.

12. h5	♖h8

This was Black's defensive idea, but *passive defense against a justified attack almost always fails.*

13. hxg6	fxg6
14. ♕h6+	♚g8

Look at the diagram below. Is one rook really enough to protect Black's lonely-looking king?

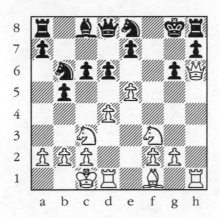

15. ♗d3! ...

Pointing most of your pieces at an underdefended king will do it every time! Incidentally, as was pointed out by two of my strongest nine-year-old students, 15. ♘g5! also wins. How? Well, to paraphrase Capablanca, "you should work this out for yourself."

15. ... ♗f5

There was no good way to stop White's threat of 16. ♗xg6!. This move fails too.

16. ♗xf5 gxf5

I don't think you have to be a "super-grandmaster" like Adams to finish Black off quickly here. You only have to attack an undefended square next to your target twice. Which one?

17. ♕e6+!	♔g7
18. ♘g5!	1-0

20. Sicilian Defense, Dragon Variation – Yugoslav Attack
Peter Winik – Damian Joseph
New York 2002

1. e4	c5
2. ♘f3	d6
3. d4	cxd4
4. ♘xd4	♘f6
5. ♘c3	g6
6. ♗e3	♗g7
7. f3	♘c6
8. ♕d2	0-0
9. ♗c4	♗d7
10. 0-0-0	♖c8
11. ♗b3	♘e5

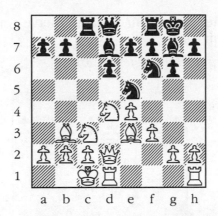

I have not said anything about the opening so far, because this position has been reached tens of thousands of times in master play, and zillions of times in games between amateurs. The standard continuation now is 12. h4 h5! (the Soltis Variation), which leads to immensely complicated play where current opening theory often extends past move twenty! *Incidentally, I recommend that intermediate-level players not use the Sicilian Dragon because it is one of those "one slip and you're dead" defenses.* White's attack pretty much plays itself, while Black finds it much harder to create counterplay.

12. ♗h6(?) ...

Inexact, as Black could have played the promising exchange sacrifice 12...♗xh6 13. ♕xh6 ♖xc3!?, typical for positions of this kind. Dragon players, and those who play against it, should always be ready to sacrifice!

12. ...	♘c4
13. ♗xc4	♖xc4
14. ♗xg7	♔xg7
15. g4	♕a5?

91

This is a waste of time. Black should have considered another promising "small" sacrifice, namely 15...b5!?. How does White nicely *combine attack and defense* now?

16. ♘b3!	♕a6
17. h4	h5?

This usually good and often essential move fails here due to a tactical trick similar to the one Adams used in the last game. What is it?

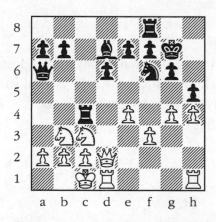

18. e5!	♘xg4!?

This counter-sacrifice is pretty much forced. Now 18...dxe5? 19. g5 loses a piece, and if Black retreats his knight then 19. gxh5 rips his kingside apart.

19. fxg4	♗xg4
20. ♖de1	♖fc8
21. exd6	exd6
22. ♖hf1	b5
23. ♕g5!	♖xc3?

White's move 23 was particularly strong and consistent – *you always want to get your power piece near the enemy king* – and it contains quite a well-concealed threat. While Black could have hung on a bit longer with 23...♖4c7 (not 23...♖8c7? because of 24. ♕f6+, followed by 25. ♖e8 mating), instead he tries one last desperate throw. How did Winik finish him off brilliantly?

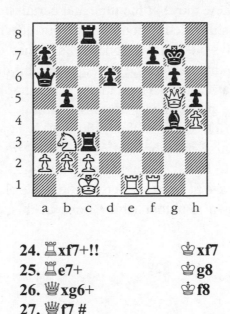

24. ♖xf7+!!	♔xf7
25. ♖e7+	♔g8
26. ♕xg6+	♔f8
27. ♕f7 #	

The following fascinating game, despite being a short "crush," is very difficult for an amateur to understand, but well worth the effort. You will learn just how much work a great player puts into his serious games before, during, and even *after* they are played!

21. Réti/English Opening
Bent Larsen – Victor Korchnoi
Brussels 1987

1. c4	♘f6
2. g3	c6
3. ♘f3	d5
4. b3	♕b6!?

This was a new move at the time and certainly an exception to the beginner's shibboleth, "don't bring your queen out early." But Korchnoi always studied his opponent's games during a tournament and knew that Larsen had already used this double-fianchetto system to defeat GM Jan Timman. As Korchnoi himself states in his two volume masterpiece, *My Best Games, Volume 2: Games with Black* (Zürich: Edition Olms, 2001), "My innovation, devised at home of course, has the aim of diverting my opponent from paths familiar to him." As an alternative to 4...♕b6!?, Korchnoi suggests 4...dxc4 5. bxc4 e5 "enlivening the play." Do you see why the e5-pawn is untouchable? Look at this variation; this is important.

5. ♗g2?!	...

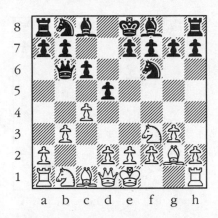

How can such a normal developing move be a mistake? Korchnoi tells us he was expecting either 5. ♗b2 dxc4 6. ♗xf6 exf6 with equality, or 5. d4 when he was intending to play an exciting gambit by 5...e5!? 6. dxe5 ♗b4+ 7. ♗d2 ♘e4, with a dangerous initiative for the pawn. What trick does 5. ♗g2? allow which gives Black exactly what he wants?

5. ...	e5!

For if 6. ♘xe5?, the *double attack* 6... ♕d4! wins a piece. Now Black has impressive center control although he is slightly behind in development. As we will see, Korchnoi clearly wanted to attack in this game and was willing to play somewhat *speculatively* while Larsen apparently could not reconcile himself to the careful, defensive play his position would require.

6. 0-0	e4
7. ♘e1	...

How can Black continue his aggression? Remember: "no guts, no glory"!

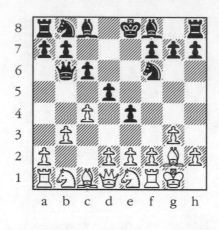

| 7. ... | h5! |
| 8. ♘c3?! | ... |

As we have learned by now, this kind of attack against a fianchetto castled position usually requires a similar move by the defender's rook pawn, so 8. h4 was the best move. Korchnoi points out in his deep, extensive annotations to this game that, "Larsen probably did not like the reply 8...♗d6 with the threat of ...♗xg3, but by continuing 9. d4, or more subtly 9. ♘c3 (9...♗xg3 10 ♘a4) White would have maintained approximate equality."

8. ...	h4
9. d4	hxg3
10. fxg3	...

While this looks safer than 10. hxg3, it limits White's possible play against Black's strong center.

| 10. ... | ♕a5!? |

Korchnoi actually gives this move an "?!" in his notes, because in analyzing it later he decided that 10...♗e6, followed by 11...

♘bd7, would give Black a "solid advantage." But I will award *you* a more positive evaluation if you chose 10...♕a5!? with a view towards possibly transferring the queen to h5 after a timely ...dxc4 (the *long, strong queen move),* creating the classic attacking ♕ + ♖ *battery* on the h-file.

11. ♕c2(?)   ...

Both Bernard Cafferty, in the June 1987 issue of *The British Chess Magazine,* and Korchnoi himself, in both *Informant* 43 (1987) and later in his game collection, believe this move to be second-rate and state that 11. ♕d2!, leaving c2 available for the knight, was best. Now how does Black continue his development with a gain of time?

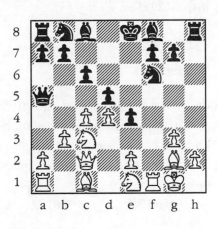

11. ...	♗b4!
12. ♗b2	♗e6
13. cxd5?	...

A serious error; after 13. a3 ♗d6 14. ♕d2! White still had good chances to resist. What did Larsen overlook?

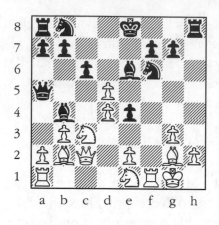

| 13. ... | ♘xd5! |

Larsen clearly missed this recapture. Even grandmasters can miss a fork (here it would be ...♘e3).

| 14. ♘xd5 | cxd5 |
| 15. a3 | ♗d2?! |

While 15...♗d6, with a dangerous initiative, is objectively stronger, this move threatens immediate destruction. Also, I think Korchnoi really "knew his customer," seeing that Larsen was having a bad day and was ripe to be finished off quickly.

| 16. ♕d1?? | ... |

A terrible blunder. 16. ♔h1, and if 16...♗e3 17. ♕c3! exchanging into an inferior endgame, was the only way to resist. Now the end comes swiftly.

| 16. ... | ♗e3+ |
| 17. ♔h1 | ... |

Black's bishop has made quite an unusual journey to reach the deadly a7-g1 diagonal (b4-d2-e3), but if White is allowed one more move he can consolidate with 18. ♘c2. How does Black administer the *coup de grâce*?

17. ...   ♛c7!
0-1

As 18...♛xg3 cannot be prevented, there is no point in White's playing on. Opening the h-file ultimately did him in!

Stop right here and don't move on to the next game yet! Please go back and set up the position from this Larsen – Korchnoi game at move four, just before White's mediocre 5. ♗g2?!. Now play through Korchnoi's superb analysis, done *after* the game, of what he discovered White should have done:

5. ♘c3! ♘e4 6. ♘xe4! dxe4 7. ♘g5 ♛d4 8. ♖b1 ♛e5 9. d4! with the better game for White (if 9...exd3 e.p. 10. ♛xd3) as he has a development advantage and will soon be harassing Black's queen.

The moral here is that if you really want to improve you must not only carefully study and re-analyze all your losses and draws from serious play, but also your victories! If you do the work, you'll reap the benefits. If you don't, you won't!

22. *Caro-Kann Defense, 5...exf6 Variation*
H. Norman-Hansen – Dr. S. Tartakower
Copenhagen 1923

1. e4		**c6**
2. d4		**d5**
3. ♘c3		**dxe4**
4. ♘xe4		**♘f6**
5. ♘xf6+		**exf6**

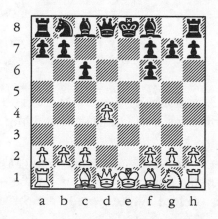

While this variation is no longer popular with grandmasters, many amateurs like it because they think their king is safe behind a wall of four pawns! And the fact that the king-and-pawn ending is lost for Black if White trades off all the pieces does not cause great concern either – this is very hard to accomplish by force. Today White's most common continuation is 6. c3 ♗d6 7. ♗d3 0-0 8. ♕c2 (with a view to queenside castling) 8...♖e8+ 9. ♘e2 with good attacking chances. Still, Norman-Hansen's *sensible setup* is also good.

6. ♘f3	♗d6
7. ♗d3	0-0
8. 0-0	♗g4
9. ♖e1	♗c7

Tartakower begins to play for tricks instead of completing his development with 9...♘d7. Actually, 9...♗c7 is not bad in itself but it is certainly the prelude to a bad idea. How would you deal with the apparent threat to White's d-pawn?

10. h3!	♗xf3?

Surprisingly Tartakower, then one of the strongest players in the world, *gets greedy* and completely underestimates his little-known opponent. Of course, 10...♗h5 was the right move.

11. ♕xf3	♕xd4??

But this is really too much! It was still not too late for Black to develop with 11...♘d7, cross his fingers, and hope that White's *bishop pair + the initiative* would not evolve into a winning advantage. I guess Black was *not really looking* that day and paid the price. How did White start him on the road to perdition?

101

12. ♖e4!		♕d5
13. c4		♕a5

White's last two moves gained him two important attacking tempos. Is there any other useful thing White can do before commencing the final attack?

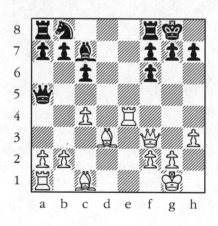

14. b4!   **...**

Deflecting Black's queen off the fifth rank so it cannot support possible defensive moves on his kingside like ...f7-f5 makes a lot of sense.

102

14. ...	♛xb4

Remembering that *sacrifices are often necessary to destroy your opponent's castled position,* how would you begin the assault?

15. ♗h6!!	...

A brilliant *passive sacrifice* which cannot be accepted (15... gxh6?? 16. ♖g4+ ♚h8 17. ♛xf6#). Black, being a *grandmaster,* finds the only way to continue, hoping he will be allowed to play 16...g6 with some chances to defend.

15. ...	♗e5

Tartakower, who was perhaps the most witty and cynical chess author, once wrote that "sacrifices only prove someone has blundered." Except here Norman-Hansen has unleashed a whole series of sacrifices since the blunder 11...♛xd4??. Is one more required?

(see diagram next page)

16. ♖xe5!	...

Removing the last defender! Black now has to run for his life.

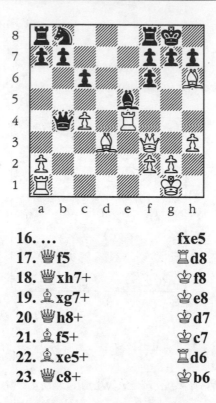

16. ...	fxe5
17. ♕f5	♖d8
18. ♕xh7+	♔f8
19. ♗xg7+	♔e8
20. ♕h8+	♔d7
21. ♗f5+	♔c7
22. ♗xe5+	♖d6
23. ♕c8+	♔b6

The game has become a classic *king hunt* and while White's last seven accurate moves have certainly driven Black to the edge, the student should be grateful that Tartakower did not give up yet. How did White continue playing with precision?

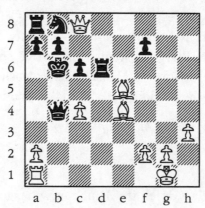

24. ♖b1!   **1-0**

24...♕xb1+ 25. ♗xb1 ♖d1+ 26. ♔h2 ♖xb1 27. ♗xb8 is an easy win. Curiously, it was Tartakower himself who first observed that "no one ever won by resigning!" but clearly here he had seen enough!

23. Scotch Four Knights
Rick Bauer – Ray Kaufman
Foxwoods Open 1999

1. e4		e5
2. ♘f3		♘c6
3. ♘c3		♘f6
4. d4		exd4
5. ♘xd4		♗b4

This common position from the Scotch Game is very important for double king pawn players to understand. After all, the Scotch is White's soundest and most fundamental attempt to take the center away from Black, and has enjoyed a tremendous resurgence in popularity since Kasparov, and soon after many others, began using it again in the 1990s. Here Black's pinning move, 5...♗b4, has created a threat to White's e-pawn. Leaving aside such beginner's blunders as 6. ♗d2?? or 6. ♗d3??, how should White answer?

6. ♘xc6	bxc6
7. ♗d3	...

White's last two moves have become standard because, of the three reasonable alternatives, both the awkward 6. ♕d3 and the logical 6. f3 allow Black to grab the initiative with 6...d5!, while after 6. ♗g5? Black forces White to give up the *bishop pair* with 6...h6! (threatening, if 7. ♗h5?, 7...g5! winning the e-pawn). Now that White has caught up in development and protected his center, what should Black do?

7. ...	d5

Seize an equal share of the center, of course! The well-intentioned mistake 7...♗xc3+?, giving White doubled, isolated pawns (though at the cost of creating serious dark-square weaknesses), was played in a national scholastic championship game about fifteen years ago with the following result: **7...♗xc3+? 8. bxc3 d5?** (8...d6 is better but after 9. ♗g5 White has pressure) **9. exd5 cxd5**

106

10. ♗a3! (White already has a winning advantage because Black's king is trapped in the center) **10...c6 11. 0-0 ♗e6 12. ♖e1 ♕d7 13. f4!** ♔d8 (13...0-0-0 loses to 14. ♗a6+, etc.) **14. f5!** (prying open the e-file) **14...♗xf5 15. ♖e7 ♕c8 16. ♖xf7 ♖g8 17. ♗xf5! ♕xf5 18. ♕e2 ♖e8 19. ♕a6! ♕e6(!)** (The best chance – and you don't want to know, as I have discovered in my classes, how many people want to play 20. ♕b7?? here, missing not only that Black gets great chances to hold on by 20...♕e3+!, but something else – what?) **20. ♕a5+!** ♔c8 **21. ♕c7#.** That's right! A mate in two missed by most of the children and adults attending the over one hundred classes in which I have used this game! You have got to remember to *always look at all your checks and captures,* and also that *sometimes you have to move backwards to attack forward!*

8. exd5	cxd5
9. 0-0	0-0
10. ♗g5	c6!

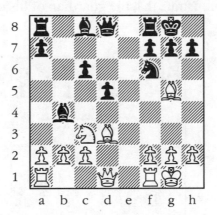

This move, which shores up the defense of d5, has been played by world champions from Steinitz in 1886 to Kasparov in 1996. It is considered to give Black equal chances in the ensuing middlegame as the most common continuations, 11. ♕f3 ♗e7 or 11. ♘e2 ♗g4, are not believed to lead to any edge for White. White's next move, introduced in the early 1990's by GM Joel Lautier, is an interesting attempt to eventually gain control of the c5 square.

11. ♘a4!	♗e6(?)

From a "master-level" point of view, this passive developing move is probably just a mistake. Better is 11...h6! because it is *always good to be able to break a pin in one move.* Now ...g7-g5 would always be available to Black if he needs it. After 12. ♗h4 ♗d6, if White tries the same plan as in this game with 13. c3, then with 13...♖e8 14. b4 ♗e5! Black has no problems.

12. c3	♗e7
13. ♗c2	♕d7
14. ♕d3	g6

Well, Black's position certainly looks pretty solid, but is there some way to demonstrate that the guardian of his dark squares may be *overloaded?*

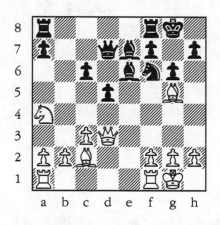

15. ♕d4! ...

A beautiful "creeping move" attacking both c5 and f6. This was

made possible because Bauer first forced the weakening move
14...g6 with his *useful* "one move threat" 14. ♕d3.

15. ...		♘g4
16. ♗xe7		♕xe7
17. ♖ae1		♕d6

How does White both attack and defend?

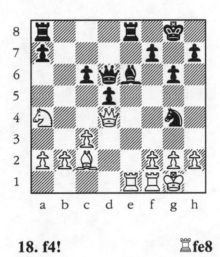

18. f4!		♖fe8

Probably Black should have just gritted his teeth and played
18...f5, though after 19. ♘c5 White is clearly much better.

19. ♘c5		♗f5?

Concerned about White's threat of f4-f5 (after 20. h3), Black
mistakenly allows his kingside to be shattered. Probably he thought
that the doubled f-pawns, controlling e4 and e5, would help him
defend along the e-file, but this turns out to be a false hope.

20. ♗xf5		gxf5
21. h3		♘h6

109

If 21...♘f6, 22. ♖e5! wins at least a pawn.

22. b4   **f6**

This is a very interesting position because, despite White's superbly placed queen and knight and much better pawn structure, I think there is only one clear way to turn his significant advantage into a winning one. What is it?

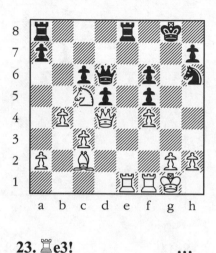

23. ♖e3!   **...**

By taking over the only open file, which Black is helpless to prevent!

23. ...	♘f7
24. ♖fe1	♖xe3
25. ♖xe3	♘d8

26. ♖e6 had to be stopped, but now White invades the eighth rank.

26. ♖e8+	♔f7
27. ♕e3	a5

Black is hanging on by his fingernails, but in reality it's all over because…?

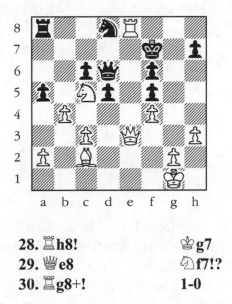

28. ♖h8!	♔g7
29. ♕e8	♘f7!?
30. ♖g8+!	1-0

I hope you didn't just grab the rook on a8 without looking because Black could then struggle on a bit longer with 30… ♘xh8.

In case you are wondering what White's "simple attacking plan" was in this game, recall that first Bauer got Black to weaken his dark squares with the clever "creeping" maneuver 14. ♕d3 and 15. ♕d4!, after which Black soon felt compelled to shatter his own kingside pawns with 19…♗f5?. Bauer then alertly seized the only open file, poured both his remaining *major pieces* into the heart of Black's position, curiously dominating the eighth rather than the seventh rank, and quickly smoked out Black's king. Sounds easy when you know how!

24. London System
Tom Schrade – Julia Kerr
New York, Bankers Athletic League, "A" Division, 2001

1. d4	d5
2. ♘f3	e6
3. ♗f4	c5
4. c3	♘c6
5. e3	♘f6
6. ♘bd2	♗e7
7. ♗d3	0-0
8. 0-0	...

I have always considered this to be a relatively insipid opening, used mainly to avoid the sharper defenses to 1. d4 such as the King's Indian, Benoni, Grünfeld, and Benko Gambit. Even Cyrus Lakdawala, in his excellent book *Play the London System* (Everyman Chess, 2010), states, "The London System is one of the safest and most solid methods of handling the white pieces." However, he also observes that, "...most Londons begin slowly and then erupt in a clash down the road, often ending with a mating attack for White."

Incidentally, either here or on the previous move Black should have considered ...♘h5, eliminating White's f4-bishop.

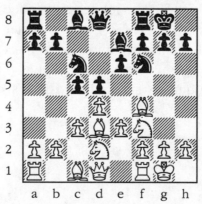

| 8. ... | ♗d7 |
| 9. ♘e5 | ♖c8? |

Tartakower once wrote, "grandmasters place their knights on e5 and then the mates come by themselves." While Tom Schrade is "only" a strong expert, he clearly understood this concept – Black should have captured on e5 before White could retake with a knight.

| 10. ♘df3 | cxd4? |

Relieving the pawn "tension" this way only helps White. The semi-open e-file will soon become a pathway for White's rooks to Black's kingside.

11. exd4	a6
12. ♖e1	b5
13. a3	h6??

A positionally horrendous move because it creates a *target* for White. Clearly Black was unfamiliar with this type of position, wasn't sure what to do, and so decided to "play it safe" by making an escape square and controlling g5. But sometimes your king is safer if the pawns in front of it remain *unmoved!* How did White now begin his attack and open another line to Black's kingside?

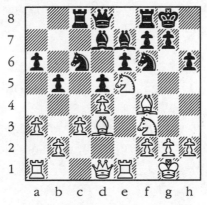

14. ♘xc6!	♗xc6
15. ♘e5	♕b6?

White's last two moves are quite purposeful: exchanging one of Black's best minor pieces (whose replacement resembles a "large pawn") and opening the d1-h5 diagonal for his queen. Maybe Black's best chance was 15...♘d7, trying to trade off one of White's attackers, rather than putting his queen on the "wrong" side of the board. At any rate, how does White get rolling?

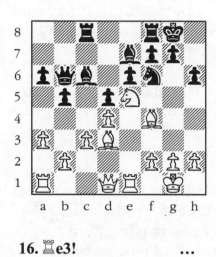

16. ♖e3! ...

An obvious and strong *rook lift,* but only the first of two (hint for later!) in this game.

16. ...	a5
17. ♖g3	♔h8

Not surprisingly, with *most of his pieces pointing at his opponent's king,* Tom finds a magnificent, deep attacking combination. What did he do?

| 18. ♗xh6!! | gxh6 |
| 19. ♕d2 | ♘g8 |

Having said "A," you must say "B." How?

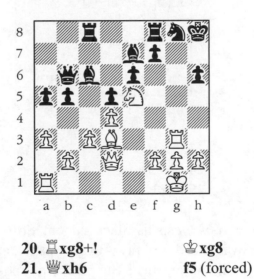

| 20. ♖xg8+! | ♔xg8 |
| 21. ♕xh6 | f5 (forced) |

It is most pleasing that Tom used both of the corollaries to our four simple attacking plans when initiating this wonderful mating attack. He essentially *sacrificed* (a full rook) *to destroy the enemy king's pawn shelter,* and this set up the *long, strong queen move* that signaled the beginning of the end! Note that Tom's next move is not to demonstrate a possible *perpetual check* but rather to force Black's king to a more vulnerable square, even further away from its protectors.

22. ♕g6+   ♚h8

The depth of Tom's calculation can only fully be appreciated now, as he also had to have seen White's next move before embarking on this adventure. What was it?

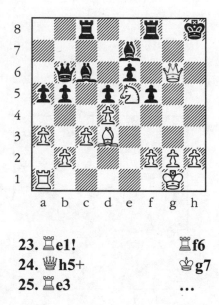

23. ♖e1!   ♜f6
24. ♕h5+   ♚g7
25. ♖e3   ...

This second *rook lift* spells Black's doom. So Tom had to calculate seven moves ahead – 14 ply – to get this far, and you can, too, if you will put in the practice! But *please* do most of your chess "workouts" in slow games using long time controls. While playing *bullet* chess on the Internet is fun, it does nothing to improve your ability to calculate long variations, rather the opposite!

25. ...   ♝d8

26. ♖g3+	♚f8

Give yourself 10 demerits if you are in a big hurry to play 27. ♕h8+?. Do not allow Black to slither away via the e7 and d6 squares, and continue to fight! Take your time, look hard and find one more good move (hint: think *trapping*).

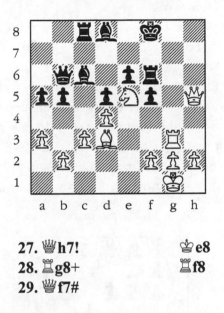

27. ♕h7!	♚e8
28. ♖g8+	♖f8
29. ♕f7#	

Although Black cooperated much too much in her own demise, this is still a beautiful and perfectly planned-out attacking game!

Footnote: When facing the London System, at least King's Indian Defense players like me usually don't have to worry about an annoying white knight (or pawn) on e5. This is because, early on, we place a pawn on d6, and, if nothing else, try never to concede control of e5 to White!

25. Four Knights' Game
J. Taubenhaus – S. Winawer
Warsaw 1900

1. e4	**e5**
2. ♘f3	**♘c6**
3. ♘c3	**♘f6**
4. ♗b5	**♗b4**
5. 0-0	**d6?**

As this old, still important, but relatively little-known game shows, this move is a mistake. Black should keep copying White's moves with 6...0-0 7. d3 d6 8. ♗g5, only breaking the symmetry now, and dealing with the threat of 9. ♘d5 by 8...♗xc3(!). This leads to a well-known position with interesting plans available for both sides. What is the most dynamic way to take advantage of 5...d6?

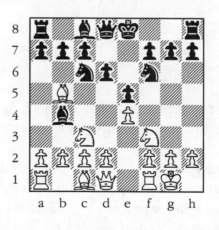

6. d4!	**exd4(?)**

Believe it or not, 6...0-0!? may be playable and I can only find a small advantage for White after 7. ♖e1. Analyze it yourself! But how can White start trouble now?

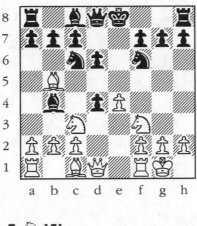

7. ♘d5! ...

Among other things, threatening to win a piece with 8. ♗xc6+ bxc6 9. ♘xb4.

7. ... ♗c5
8. ♗g5 ♗d7
9. ♖e1 ...

Don't be in a big hurry to take on f6. Remember that *your rook always belongs on the file opposite an uncastled king.*

9. ... a6

Trying to relieve some of the pressure, but can you see how White blasts the position open?

(see diagram next page)

10. e5! dxe5

On 10...axb5 11. exf6+ ♗e6 12. fxg7 White wins.

11. ♘xe5! ...

119

Threatening a crushing *discovered check*. If 11...0-0, then 12. ♗xf6 gxf6 13. ♘xd7 and, to quote Irving Chernev, "Black's whole position is *en prise.*"

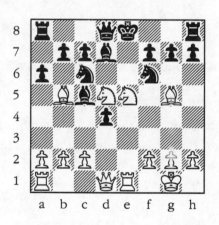

11. ...	♘xe5
12. ♖xe5+	♔f8
13. ♘xf6	gxf6
14. ♗h6+	♔g8

Now that you have trapped Black's king, what is the most precise finish?

15. ♕f3!   **1-0**

A quick mate on the g-file cannot be prevented.

26. Four Knights' Game
G. Maróczy – C. von Bardeleben
Barmen 1905

1. e4	e5
2. ♘f3	♘c6
3. ♘c3	♘f6
4. ♗b5	♗c5
5. 0-0	d6?

As in the previous game, in a very similar position, this normal-looking move is a mistake. In fact, the "book" move is 5...0-0, and then White's strongest continuation is 6. ♘xe5! ♘xe5 (6...♖e8 is also possible) 7. d4 ♗d6 8. f4! ♘c6 9. e5, leading to a very complex position believed to favor White. If you want to play the Four Knights' Game you will have to study this variation. But here, how can White attack the center while Black is still not castled and his c6-knight is pinned?

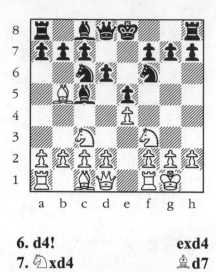

6. d4!	**exd4**
7. ♞xd4	**♝d7**

Now what? How can you force open the e-file?

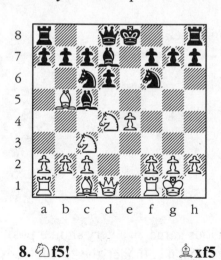

8. ♞f5!	**♝xf5**

Besides the game continuation, GM Maróczy had to calculate what he would do on 8...0-0. Take your time and give it a shot! OK, if 8...0-0 9. ♝g5 h6 10. ♝h4 ♚h7 11. ♞xg7! ♚xg7 12. ♞d5 ♝d4 13. c3; while 9...♝xf5 10. exf5 ♞d4 11. ♝d3 d5 12. ♝xf6 gxf6 13. ♞a4! b6 (13...♝b6 loses to 14. ♞xb6 followed by

15. ♕g4+) 14. b4! ♕d7 15. c3 wins a piece. It is interesting how frequently different *pins* restrict Black's decision-making in this game.

9. exf5	**♘d7**
10. ♖e1+	**♘de5**

Black has cleverly contrived to block the e-file and hopes to escape with a whole skin. How should White proceed?

11. ♘a4!	**...**

By forcing the exchange of Black's best minor piece (which is preventing f2-f4 winning the e5-knight), thus gaining the *bishop pair* in an open position, White achieves a significant advantage.

11. ...	**0-0 (forced)**
12. ♘xc5	**dxc5**

Has Black gotten away or can White force the win of at least a pawn?

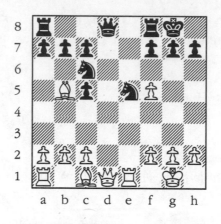

13. ♗e3! ...

Maróczy, one of the strongest players at the beginning of the 20th century, offers his opponent a chess version of "Hobson's choice": either accept a poor endgame with 13...♕xd1 14. ♖axd1, where, at a minimum, Black will lose the c5-pawn (for if 14...b6?, then 15.f4! and one of the knights is lost), or...?

13. ... **♕f6??**

...or avoid this bad ending by blundering away a piece instead! What did Black forget?

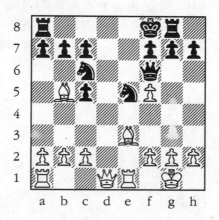

14. f4!	...

That his knight is short of squares and will be trapped!

14. ...	♖fd8
15. fxe5	♘xe5
16. ♕h5	c4
17. b3	c3
18. ♕g5	♕d6
19. f6	1-0

I hope you noticed that Maróczy was willing to trade the pressure he had created on the e-file in the opening for a transition into a probably winning endgame. Recognizing the necessity to be flexible – when you must consider exchanging one type of advantage for another – is the hallmark of strong, strategic play. Not infrequently, strong opponents will try to deflect your simple and dangerous attacking plan by offering you a transposition of your advantage(s) in the opening or middlegame into a better endgame. And, often, you had better take it!

While we're talking about the very important concept of *transformation of advantages,* let me now show you a game where *I improved upon Capablanca* in the opening (I bet that got your attention)!

27. Four Knights' Game
F. Wilson – Bob O'Keefe
New York 2001

1. e4	e5
2. ♘f3	♘c6
3. ♘c3	...

I like the Four Knights' Game very much and have played it consistently now for about fifteen years. I also think using the Four Knights against opponents of less than master or expert strength is virtually a license to steal! This is because it has been generally ignored and/or underestimated by the avalanche of trendy opening books that have come out during the last decade, and many less-experienced players have little or no practice on Black's side of it.

Black's next move is a common mistake.

3. ...   ♝ **c5?**

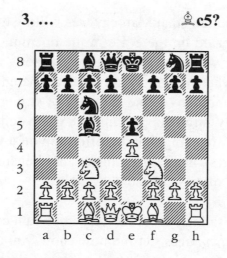

Even if your knowledge of the *classical* openings is sorely lacking, you should be able to find the "trick" White has here.

4. ♘xe5   **...**

This is your basic *fork trick* and it has been around forever. The best continuation for Black here is 4...♘xe5 5. d4 ♗d6 6. dxe5 ♗xe5, retaining the bishop, although after White plays 7. ♗d3 followed by 0-0 and f2-f4 he has a space and development advantage. Once in a while you will surprise a strong opponent with 4. ♘xe5 here and, after recovering from the shock, they will, like Bob O'Keefe (a tough, expert-strength player in NYC's Bankers League), go into a long think and play the following dangerous-looking albeit ultimately incorrect move.

4. ...	♗xf2+(?)

A seductive move as White's king seems exposed and he has lost the right to castle. But White has the *bishop pair* and will soon control most of the center. He just has to be careful if Black, after...

5. ♔xf2	♘xe5
6. d4	...

...tries the tricky 6...♕f6+ 7. ♔g1 ♘g4!? threatening mate, for if 8. ♕xg4??, then 8...♕xd4+ and mate next move! In fact, you had better play over this variation because White has only one correct response! Can you find it?

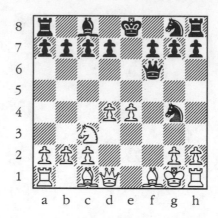

8. ♕d2! covers all the bases, and after 9.h3 White will have a big edge.

However, Bob rejected this line during his long think – he didn't believe a master would fall for it – and played, relatively speaking, the best move.

6. ...   ♘g6(!)

I did remember Capablanca had this position a couple of times, that it is also good for White, and so (full disclosure!) without *thinking it through,* quickly decided that my bishop was better placed on d3 than c4, pointing at h7 for an upcoming middlegame attack. In fact, Capa played 7. ♗c4 against Randolph at New York 1912, but after 7…d6 8. ♖f1 ♗e6! 9. ♗xe6 fxe6 10. ♔g1 ♘f6 11. ♗g5 0-0 12. ♕d3 ♕d7 13. ♗xf6 ♖xf6 14. ♖xf6 gxf6 15. ♖f1 ♖f8 16. ♕b5 c6 17. ♕b3 d5 18. exd5 cxd5 Black is still hanging in there.

7. ♗d3!?   ...

At this point Bob started thinking hard again, and during the 6-8 minutes that passed I noticed to my horror that he could win a pawn! And, sure enough he played…

7. ...   ♛f6+!

...but what forcing, tempo-gaining four-move sequence had I prepared while thinking on Bob's time?

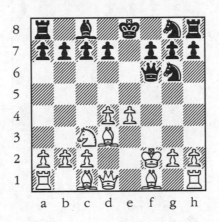

8. ♕f3!	♛xd4+
9. ♗e3	♛f6
10. ♘d5!	♛xf3+
11. gxf3!	♚d8 (forced)

You may be wondering what this game has to do with the concept of *transformation of advantages*. Think about 10. ♘d5! and decide, if Black declines the queen trade by 10...♛d8, whether or not White has sufficient compensation in development and attacking potential for the sacrificed pawn. I think he does. Now had I made this pawn "sac" (7. ♗d3!?) *intentionally* (which I swear I will do if I'm ever given another opportunity!), I would have had to envision this exact endgame arising, believing as I did and still do that White's compensation for the sacrificed pawn is substantial. What you will see for the remainder of this game is a good illustration of the famous chess motto, *"attack where you are strongest."* Black's kingside is quite vulnerable and it is not relevant that his king is located elsewhere. How do you begin to train your guns on the kingside and begin a powerful *positional attack*?

12. ♗d4!	f6
13. h4	c6

Do you have to pay attention to this threat or can you make a bigger one? (I know I sound like a "broken record" but buying into this idea is vital to becoming a good player.)

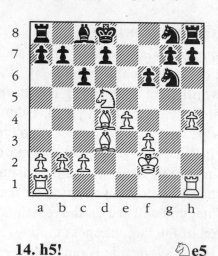

14. h5!	♘e5

14...cxd5? 15. hxg6 h6 (15...dxe4? 16. ♖xh7! and White wins) 16. exd5 drops a pawn.

15. ♘f4	♘e7
16. ♖ag1	♖g8
17. c3	d5?

Black's last move is a mistake because I don't think he noticed I wanted to reroute the light-squared bishop to the a2-g8 diagonal. To quote IM John Donaldson, who briefly annotated this game in *Inside Chess Online*, "Here 17...♘xd3 must be played, but after 18. ♘xd3 White will double on the g-file, winning his pawn back with some advantage."

18. ♗c2!	g5 (desperation)
19. hxg6	hxg6
20. exd5	cxd5
21. ♖h7	♗d7

Black's position is holding together by a thread. How can you push it to the breaking point?

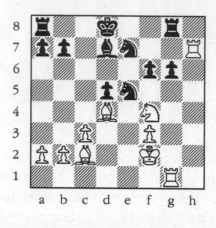

22. ♖e1!   **...**

Honest to God, this was the most difficult move of the game for me! But once I understood that only the e5-knight was holding Black's game together, it was easy to find.

22. ...   **♘7c6(?)**

Black "hangs" the d5-pawn but he had no good move.

23. ♘xd5	**♖f8**
24. ♗c5	**♖f7**
25. ♖h8+	**♗e8**

Why was 25. ♖h8+ much stronger than winning a pawn by 25. ♖xf7?

| | 26. ♗xg6! | ... |

A *petite combinaison* as the bishop cannot be captured.

	26. ...	♘e7
	27. ♗xf7	♘d3+
	28. ♔e2	1-0

You may still be wondering why this game was included, but think about it: didn't White attack where he was strongest, targeting Black's kingside, particularly the squares g7 and h7? After crashing through at h7, didn't White's vastly superior center control lead to a decisive gain of material? About the only thing missing from this consistent, aggressively played game is a direct attack on Black's king! And still Black's awkwardly placed monarch, interfering with the coordination of his pieces, certainly hastened his doom. It is therefore important to remember that sometimes the correct simple attacking plan need not involve a direct attack on your opponent's king. Witness the following very lightly annotated game from my youth – which I am still proud of – to see what I mean.

28. Philidor's Defense
F. Wilson – Koppel
New York 1966

1. e4	d6
2. d4	e5
3. dxe5	dxe5
4. ♕xd8+	♚xd8
5. ♗c4	f6

Believe it or not, nowadays 5...♗e6!? is often played here, as the endgame after 6. ♗xe6 fxe6 is considered viable by many masters. The isolated, doubled e-pawns are hard to get at, and do control important squares. This is why today I would play 3. ♘f3, angling towards a more standard Philidor's or Old Steinitz Defense to the Ruy López, rather than allowing an "instant" endgame.

6. ♘c3	c6
7. ♗e3	♘d7
8. 0-0-0	♚c7
9. f4	♗d6
10. g3	♘b6
11. ♗b3	♗g4
12. ♖d2	♖d8
13. h3	♗c8

White wants to develop his knight to f3 but Black's problem is that he cannot insert 13...exf4, with the idea of 14. gxf4 ♗h5, because then White wins a piece with 14. ♗xb6+!. Also, 13...♗h5 lets White advance on the kingside, *where he is stronger,* with 14. g4, etc.

14. ♘f3	♘e7

15. a3	♖hf8

While 15. a3 was not strictly necessary (the pin on the knight by 15...♗b4 should not be feared), now White has to make an important decision. What is it?

16. f5!	...

Lock him up on the kingside, advance down the g- and h-files, and plan to crash through on either g7 or h7, which should eventually win material. Sound familiar?

16. ...	♘g8
17. g4	♗e7
18. ♖xd8	♔xd8

Control of the d-file is no longer important.

19. g5	♔c7
20. h4	♘d7
21. h5	♗c5
22. ♗xc5	♘xc5

135

Black has been seeking relief through exchanges, but it is too late! Now comes a simple but devastating liquidation eliminating a key defender. What is it?

(Anyone who wanted to play either 23. g6? or 24. g6?, allowing Black to totally block the kingside with…h7-h6, please leave the room!)

23. ♗xg8!	♖xg8
24. ♖g1!	♖d8

Black is trying to defend laterally but this fails to an instructive breakthrough.

25. h6!	♖d7

Hoping for 26. hxg7 ♖xg7 27. gxf6 ♖xg1+ 28. ♘xg1, when after 28…♔d6! Black can fight on. However, after…

26. g6!	…

…which makes quite a pretty picture, it's all over.

26. ...	hxg6
27. h7	♖d8
28. ♖xg6	♖h8
29. ♖xg7+	♔b6
30. ♘h4!	1-0

The following serves as sort of a very cute corollary to my 1966 game. Here IM Jay Bonin not only improves on my play with his early 6. f4!, he also demonstrates once again that a king trapped in the center, even in a queenless middlegame, can fall prey to an onslaught from *all your pieces!*

29. Philidor's Defense
Jay Bonin – Boris Privman
New York 2000

1. d4 d6 2. e4 e5 3. dxe5 dxe5 4. ♕xd8+ ♔xd8 5. ♗c4 f6 6. f4! ♗d6 7. fxe5 ♗xe5? 8. ♘f3 ♗d6? (with hindsight, giving up the *bishop pair* with 8...♘d7 was safer) **9. ♘c3 c6 10. ♗e3 ♘e7 11. 0-0-0 ♔c7** (You must act now! How?)

137

12. ♖xd6!! ♔xd6 13. ♖d1+! (not 13. ♗f4+ first because after 13...♔d7 Black can slink away to e8) **13...♔c7 14. ♗f4+ ♔b6 15. ♘a4+ ♔a5 16. ♗d2+! ♔xa4 17. ♘d4! 1-0** "Tap city," as 18. ♗b3# cannot be stopped.

30. Sicilian Defense, Rossolimo Variation
S. Galdunts – F. Katz
Calvi 2004

1. e4	**c5**
2. ♘f3	**♘c6**
3. ♗b5	**♕b6**

Today 3...g6 4. ♗xc6 dxc6 is all the rage. This early queen move is not very popular.

4. ♘c3	**e6**

Perhaps the only thing wrong with Black's position is that he lags slightly behind in development.

5. 0-0		♞ge7
6. ♖e1		♞d4
7. a4!		...

A good move, not only stifling Black's potential play on the queenside, but also forcing him to make an important decision...

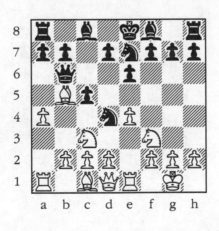

7. ...	♞xb5?

...which should have been to ignore the bishop and continue developing! Black should have played 7...a6 8. ♗c4 ♞g6 9. d3 with only a small advantage for White. Exchanging his best-placed piece for a not particularly important bishop – which is now replaced by quite a cramping pawn – was not a good idea. Also, it weakens his control of the d4 square, which will become important later on.

8. axb5!	**d6**
9. d4!	**...**

What? You probably thought White wanted to avoid playing an "open" Sicilian, didn't you? But remember, when an opponent plays as "pokey" as Black has here, and is seriously underdeveloped, then *you want to open the center files*.

9. ...	**♗d7**
10. dxc5	**dxc5**

How to proceed? Hint: move forward while making threats!

11. ♘e5!	**♕d8**

Unfortunately forced, as after 11...♖d8? 12. ♘c4! wins hands down.

12. ♗g5!   f6?

Honestly, I hope you prepared for this possible reply. While Black really doesn't have a good move here, this hastens the end. How can you set up a killing *long, strong queen move?*

13. ♗xf6!   gxf6
14. ♕h5+   ♘g6
15. ♘xg6   hxg6
16. ♕xg6+   ♔e7

Now you've got him on the ropes. Find the crusher!

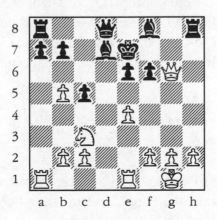

17. ♘d5+!	exd5

If 17...♚d6, then 18. ♕g3+ e5 19. ♖ad1 does the trick.

18. exd5+	♝e6

Because 18...♚d6?? allows 19. ♕g3+ ♚xd5 20. ♕d3#.

19. ♖xe6+	♚d7
20. ♕f7+	1-0

For if 20...♝e7 (20...♚c8 21. ♖e8), then 21. ♖ae1 ♖e8 22. d6 is hopeless.

31. King's Indian Defense
Kayden Troff – Daniel Naroditsky
U.S. Junior Closed Championship,
St. Louis 2011

1. d4	g6
2. c4	♝g7

White, a 12-year-old master (!) from Utah, declines to make the opening a Pirc/Modern Defense with 2. e4. It is interesting that two of the strongest 1. d4 players of my generation, GMs Anatoly Karpov and Walter Browne, never missed the opportunity to do so.

3. ♘c3	d6
4. e4	♘f6
5. f4	...

This is the Four Pawns' Attack, which – while not the most testing variation against the King's Indian – can be quite dangerous.

Usually Black here plays either 5…c5 or, more often, 5…0-0 6. ♘f3 c5, which can lead to somewhat Sicilian Dragon-like positions unless White closes the center with 7. d5. I personally like 5…0-0 6. ♘f3 ♘a6 7. ♗e2 e5!?, which is quite complicated and less explored.

5. ...   **♗g4!?**

However, I was unable to find IM Naroditsky's move in any of the editions of *Modern Chess Openings* or the *Encyclopedia of Chess Openings* that I consulted! So much for there being "nothing new under the sun"! It is clear Black either wanted to trade the light-squared bishops after 6. ♗e2, or was willing, after 6. ♘f3 0-0 7. ♗e2 ♘6d7! (targeting d4) 8. ♗e3 ♗xf3 9. ♗xf3 (9. gxf3 e5! 10. fxe5 dxe5 11. d5 ♗h6! with complications favoring Black) 9…♘c6 10. d5 ♘a5!?, to transpose into a variation popular in the 1970s now thought to give White a slight advantage.

6. ♕b3?   **...**

Unfortunately for Troff, he innovates. What is wrong with his one-move threat?

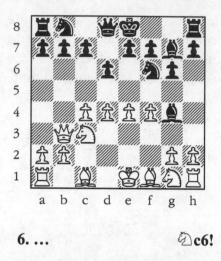

6. ... ♘c6!

It can be ignored! The whole point of the King's Indian Defense is to take control of the dark squares e5 and d4, by force if necessary. Study and learn how relentlessly well Black does it here.

7. ♗e3 e5!
8. ♕xb7 ...

This is the key position in the game. No doubt you prepared something for this eventuality, right? How did Black strike first?

8. ...	exd4!

*Things fall apart; the center cannot hold
Mere anarchy is loosed upon the board.*
(with apologies to W. B. Yeats)

Actually, White has simply been out-calculated as he clearly didn't see that Black could leave his knight hanging with check. Now 9. ♕xc6+ ♗d7 10. ♕a6 (or 10. ♕b7) 10...dxc3 leaves White's center control and dark squares in shreds.

9. ♘b5	0-0

White loses the knight if he plays 10. ♘xc7?. You can figure it out yourself.

10. ♕xc6	dxe3
11. ♘c3	...

Now find the surprising winning move.

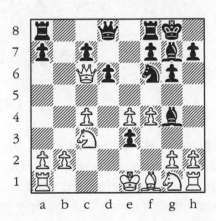

11. ...	♖b8!

145

The point is that b2 cannot be defended: 12. b3? fails to 12...♘xe4!, while 12. ♖b1 runs into 12...♖b6 13. ♕a4 ♘h5! threatening, among other things, 14...♗xc3+. White attempts a radical solution to his problems, hoping to keep his center intact at the expense of the b-pawn.

12. ♗e2!?	♖xb2
13. 0-0-0	♕b8
14. h3	...

Castling into a semi-open file dominated by an enemy battery doesn't look very safe. How did Black exploit the White defender that is *overloaded?*

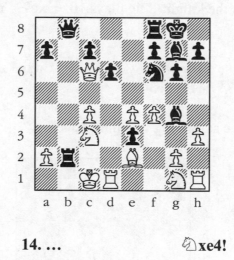

14. ...	♘xe4!

Pow! The knight can't protect both b1 and e4. It is curious that since White's mistaken queen sortie on move five, attacking the *queen knight pawn,* his impressive center has been completely destroyed. No wonder Dr. Siegbert Tarrasch (one of the first five original grandmasters) wrote that, "he who takes the b-pawn sleeps in the streets"!

Now the end comes quickly.

15. ♘xe4	♖b1+
16. ♔c2	♕b2+
17. ♔d3	♕a3+?!

I don't mean to be picky as this wins easily, but can you spot the mate in three here (missed by myself and about a dozen other people attending my lecture, "Think Outside the Bun. How to Create and Implement Surprising Attacking Schemes," held at my chess bookstore on August 19, 2011)?

Answer: 17...♖xd1+ 18. ♗xd1 ♕d4+! 19. ♔c2 ♕xd1#. Naroditsky and the rest of us just forgot the g7-bishop still owns those dark squares!

18. ♘c3	♕xc3+
19. ♔e4	f5+
20. ♔d5	♖xd1+
0-1	

By the way, I hope you noticed that after 14...♘xe4! Naroditsky had *nearly all his pieces pointed at his opponent's king!* And, analogous to having an open g-file down which to attack when storming the kingside, in this game the b-file was the path to destruction.

32. Modern Defense
Jon Ludvig Hammer – Magnus Carlsen
World Youth Championship (Under 14), Halkidiki 2003

| 1. ♘f3 | d6 |

It is interesting that even at 12 years of age Carlsen, currently (in 2012) the highest-rated player in the world, was willing to play a Pirc

Defense when White was precluded from playing the very aggressive systems against it requiring the early pawn advance f3 or f4.

2. d4	♘f6
3. ♘bd2	g6
4. e4	♗g7

It is important for inveterate King's Indian players to understand that this position can be reached via the move order 1. d4 ♘f6 2. ♘f3 g6 3. ♘bd2, and now instead of preventing 4. e4 with 3...d5, they can allow White to play this relatively insipid system against the Pirc where Black can often create exciting counterplay.

5. ♗d3	0-0
6. 0-0	♘c6

In general, I prefer putting this knight on c6, attacking d4 and e5, rather than the more passive d7 square. In the event of 7. d5, simply 7... ♘e5 8. ♘xe5 dxe5 and Black will soon dissolve the doubled pawn.

7. c3	e5
8. h3(?)	...

This is unnecessary as 8...♗g4 was not really a threat (in that case then simply 9. h3). In fact, it costs an important tempo that should have been spent on the genuinely useful move 8. ♖e1.

8. ...	♘h5!

Threatening 9...♘f4. Had White played 8. ♖e1 instead of 8. h3, he could have replied 9. dxe5 dxe5 10. ♘f1, and been ready to capture the knight on 10...♘f4.

9. dxe5	...

To quote GM Simen Agdestein in his excellent book about the young Carlsen, *Wonderboy* (New in Chess, 2004), how is it possible here that "Magnus can already chase the initiative"?

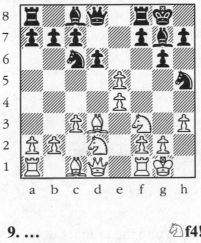

9. ...	♘f4!
10. ♗b5	♘xe5
11. ♘xe5	...

For the second time in three moves, you should ask yourself the question, "must I recapture immediately?"

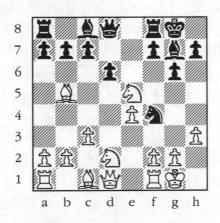

11. ...	♕g5!

Not when you can threaten mate!

12. ♘g4	♛xb5
13. ♘b3	♘e2+!

A bold move; Magnus had to calculate that his knight would not get trapped.

14. ♔h1	♝xg4
15. hxg4	♖ae8!

To quote GM Agdestein again: "Black has evil plans."

16. ♝e3?	...

White thinks he can trap the knight but he is quite mistaken. 16. a4 ♛a6 would have prolonged the struggle.

16. ...	♖xe4
17. ♖e1??	...

The final blunder. 17. g3 is required, though 17...♘xg3+! should win easily enough. Considering that the white king has almost no *flight squares,* what should you look for?

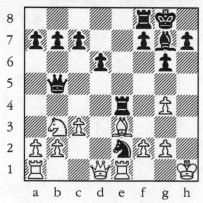

17. ...	♕h5+!

How to put him in check! **0-1**

Now that's a *long, strong queen move!*

To round off our selection on how to create attacking schemes via King's Indian setups, enjoy (and study!) the following win by White.

33. *King's Indian Attack*
Esther Epstein (USA) – Narcisa Mihevc (Slovenia)
International Chess Olympiad
Elista 1998

1. e4	c5
2. ♘f3	e6
3. d3	...

This introduces the King's Indian Attack, also known as the King's Indian Reversed. It is quite popular against Paulsen Sicilian setups (1. e4 c5 2. ♘f3 e6) and was often used by Bobby Fischer.

3. ...	♘c6
4. g3	g6

4...d5 leads to an entirely different type of middlegame for which Fischer – Myagmarsuren (Sousse 1967) and Kaidanov – Nijboer, also from Elista 1998, are two classic attacking examples from White's viewpoint.

5. ♗g2	♗g7
6. 0-0	♘ge7

7. ♖e1	d5
8. ♘bd2	0-0

GM John Fedorowicz was the coach of the U.S. Women's team during this Olympiad. In his superb article about this event, "China Thwarts U.S. in Bid for Gold" *(Chess Life,* Dec. 1998, pp. 34-46), John writes while annotating this game that, "In preparation we looked at this exact position. Black should delay castling."

How can White begin the process of "softening up" Black's kingside?

9. h4!	**b6**

Black could have prevented White's next move by playing 10... h5 herself, but then the respective weaknesses on g4 and g5 would favor White (who can occupy Black's weak square, g5, first).

10. h5	♗b7
11. hxg6	**hxg6**

What undefended square near Black's king do you want to target, and how should you do so?

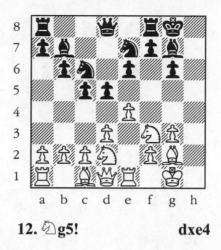

12. ♘g5!   **dxe4**

That's right, h7! See how consistently White follows up this *simple attacking plan*.

           13. dxe4   **♕c7**
           14. ♘f1   **♖ad8?**

The wrong rook as 14...♖fd8, besides seizing the d-file, also saves a tempo while creating a possibly useful flight square for the black king.

           15. ♕g4   **♘b4(?)**

An empty threat, though Black's position is already badly compromised.

           16. ♕h4   **♖fe8**
           17. ♘e3   **♘c8**
           18. a3   **♘c6**

And now, how do you point more of your pieces at Black's king (don't forget that the apparently undeveloped c1-bishop is already "working")?

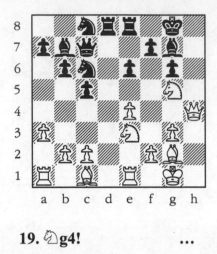

19. ♘g4! ...

To quote "Fed" again, "Now it's too late for a defense."

19. ... ♘d4

Black repeats her earlier threat from a different square but it's way too late now. Remembering the theme of our *simple attacking plan,* can you find and accurately calculate White's forced win? (Hint: invade the target with the correct piece!)

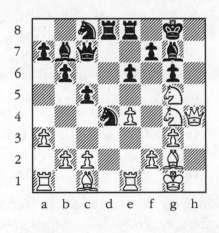

20. ♘h7! ♘xc2

21. ♘gf6+	♝xf6
22. ♘xf6+	♚f8
23. ♗h6+	1-0

If 23...♚e7, then 24. ♘d5++ with *double check* is crushing.

The following game is quite reminiscent of Rossolimo – Winser, Hastings 1950 (Game 5). You will see similar pawn structures, piece development, errors in judgment by the loser. Even White's explosive winning combination will be detonated on the same square. But enough hints: sit back, relax, enjoy, and study this neglected masterpiece by GM Robert Hess, currently the fourth-highest rated player in the United States (as of August, 2012), amazingly played when he was not quite yet 14 years old (!).

34. Scandinavian Defense
Robert Hess – Wouter Spoelman
World Youth Championship (Under 14),
Crete 2004

1. e4	d5
2. exd5	♕xd5
3. ♘c3	♕d6!?

This variation of the Scandinavian seems to be all the rage these days, especially with those players seeking to play a Caro-Kann-like defense with a bit more bite. In *Scandinavian Defense: The Dynamic 3...♛d6,* 2nd edition (Russell Enterprises, Inc., 2009) by Michael Melts, the author points out that, "The move 3...♛d6 has its pluses and minuses, as does (the traditional) 3...♛a5." He goes on to elaborate that the position of the black queen on a5 is just as vulnerable to an eventual b2-b4 or ♗d2 by White, as it is on d6 where it may be harassed by an eventual ♘b5 or ♗f4. "You pays your money and you takes your choice" – but, frankly, I don't personally believe in either version of this active, but tempo-losing defense.

4. d4	♘f6
5. ♘f3	a6
6. ♗e3	e6

In an analogous position, without 5...a6 and 6. ♗e3, Melts recommends 5...♗g4, and if now 6. ♗e3 then either 6...c6 or 6...a6. Curiously, I cannot find the normal-looking position that occurred here anywhere in Melts's 301-page (double-column, smallish print!) book on this defense. Which only goes to prove both sides can still play six sensible opening moves and achieve a reasonable position that is still relatively unexplored territory!

7. ♗e2	♘bd7
8. 0-0	b5?

I believe that this is a mistake and the beginning of a surprisingly fast, bad trip down a long, slippery slope. Black should not have neglected his king's safety, and instead should have played 8...♗e7 followed by ...0-0. Perhaps he decided to play somewhat riskily because of the significant rating edge he had over Hess (2357 to 2214), forgetting something all chess coaches know full well: that *all strong kids are underrated!*

Now I'm going to ask you to think about the following position for a while. Don't look for a good move, find a good *plan* instead. Remember that this plan should include trying to challenge Black's seemingly secure control of the light squares in the center with a view towards cracking open the e- and d-files to get at the uncastled king.

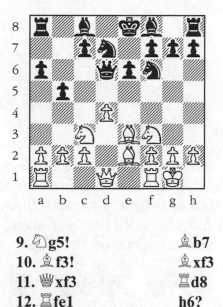

9. ♘g5!	♗b7
10. ♗f3!	♗xf3
11. ♕xf3	♖d8
12. ♖fe1	h6?

12...♗e7 was Black's last chance to get his king out of the center alive, though 13. d5 e5 14. ♖ad1 certainly looks promising. How did Hess respond to this threat?

(see diagram next page)

13. ♗f4! ...

By ignoring it and making a bigger one! (I cannot overemphasize the importance of this concept.) Black may as well grab the d-pawn and have something for his suffering.

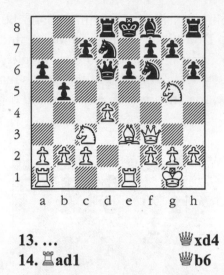

| 13. ... | ♕xd4 |
| 14. ♖ad1 | ♕b6 |

Try to really think outside the box here. Consider Black's vulnerabilities: king stuck in the center, pressure down both central files, and on f7 and e6 (which is pinned), Black's queen is on a dark square which can be easily attacked – there, have I given you enough hints to find the brilliant breakthrough?

15. ♘d5!!	♘xd5
16. ♘xf7!	♔xf7
17. ♗xc7+	♔g8

18. ♗xb6	♘7xb6

Now you must revert back from the *sacred* (sacrificing) to the *profane* (materialism). How did White – after this superb combination – cash in by converting energy into matter?

19. ♖xe6! ...

White is simply winning a piece back because of the pin on the d-file. He now finishes accurately. A wonderful game!

19. ...	♘f4
20. ♖xb6	♖xd1+
21. ♕xd1	♔h7
22. ♕f3	♗c5
23. ♕e4+	1-0

Eliminating the defender of a square crucial to your success is one of the most important tactical concepts you need to master if you want to become a good player. Here is a slightly revised version of an essay I wrote for my students on this essential idea about a decade ago. It is illustrated with a truly neglected masterpiece.

DEFLECTION, UNDERMINING,
OR REMOVING THE GUARD?

I have noticed over the years a surprising lack of consensus among chess teachers, chess authors – indeed chessplayers in general – regarding the definitions of standard tactical themes. For example, we all know (or should know) that a *fork* and a *double attack* are essentially the same thing. When this attack on two units simultaneously by a single chessman is carried out by a knight or a pawn, we usually call this tactic a *fork*. However, when this tactic is effected by a bishop, rook, or queen we usually call it a *double attack*!

Also, I have found a surprising lack of consistency within the chess community when discussing the extremely important tactic involving the removal or elimination of a defender. I have most often found this kind of tactic described as either *deflection, undermining,* or *removing the guard*, with about equal frequency. Fred Reinfeld, in his classic *1001 Brilliant Chess Sacrifices and Combinations* (1955), when discussing *removing the guard*, points out that, "the principle underlying this theme is the very essence of chess logic. If Piece A guards Piece B, then attack Piece A and you win one or the other." He further adds that, "removing the guard is one of the most useful of all the tactical themes. In chess, there is no surer winning method than concentrating on hostile units that are tied down to some vital task." Later on, in *Pandolfini's Chess Complete* (1992) my colleague Bruce Pandolfini defines *removing the defender* as "a tactic making a unit vulnerable by capturing, luring or driving away, or immobilizing its protector. Also called removing the guard or undermining." And in Patrick Wolff's superb *The Complete Idiot's Guide to Chess* (1995), he states, "deflection refers to when one piece is forced to move away from a square where it is needed for some reason." Interestingly, M.V. Blokh, in his famous masterpiece about chess tactics, *The Art of Combination* (1994), uses none of the three most common ways for describing *removing the defender* but instead refers to this concept by the fearsome phrase *annihilation of defense*.

While I could give countless examples, I think you get the idea: there is no agreement among chess writers regarding standard definitions of many fundamental tactical concepts. No matter what you call this tactical operation – *deflection, undermining,* or *removing the guard* – I would add to its definitions that *to carry it out successfully, you must eliminate your opponent's control of a square vital to his safety.*

The position after Black's move 20 in the following game is perhaps the most difficult combination to solve in this book. It is not so hard because of its length, but rather because of the difficulty in discerning what square in Black's position White needs to undermine. I discovered this virtually unknown masterpiece while browsing through the August 1965 issue of *Chess Review*, a great periodical that ran from 1933 to 1969. I know of no electronic databases nor published games collections that contain the following brilliancy by IM Walter Shipman (who is still an active force on the California chess scene).

35. Scandinavian Defense
Walter Shipman (Manhattan Chess Club) –
Louis Levy (Marshall Chess Club)
New York City, Metropolitan Chess League 1965

1. e4   **d5**

I should point out that while this opening is no longer used much by top grandmasters, it is extremely popular with amateurs who like dynamic piece activity.

2. exd5		♕xd5	
3. ♘c3		♕a5	
4. d4		♘f6	
5. ♗c4		c6	
6. ♘ge2!		...	

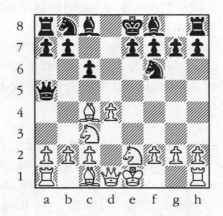

White's standard move is 6. ♘f3, which leads to several long, deeply analyzed variations that are quite complex. I am recommending here a little-known sideline that is generally neglected or even completely ignored by current opening literature. It has been championed in recent years by the well-respected openings theoretician GM Mikhail Golubev, and it has often been played successfully by him and other grandmasters such as McShane, Shabalov, and Movsesian.

6. ...		e6

For the apparently more active 6...♗f5, see the supplemental game Kristol – Morozova that follows this one. I think Levy, a strong master, carefully examined Black's potential problems after 7. ♘g3, followed by an early advance of White's f-pawn, and decided to "play it safe." Although he does achieve a position akin to the solid Caro-Kann Defense, I believe Black has lost time with his queen and should be slightly worse.

Interestingly, GM John Emms in his excellent book *The Scandinavian,* 2nd edition (Everyman Chess, 2004), even suggests 5...♗g4!? instead of 5...c6 as Black's most accurate move, with a view towards possible queenside castling after 6. f3 ♗f5 7. ♘ge2 e6 8. 0-0 ♘bd7.

Back to our game. After Levy's "safe" 6...e6, how does Shipman, with a simple developing move, take away Black's best square for his queen?

7. ♗f4!	♘bd7
8. 0-0	♗e7
9. ♕d2!	...

Shipman sets a nice trap. Do you see it?

After the apparently safe 9...0-0 10. ♘d5! ♕d8 11. ♘xe7+ ♕xe7 12. ♗g5, White has a clear advantage.

| 9. ... | ♕b4 |

Hans Kmoch, writing in *Chess Review* (August 1965), observes that, "Black's queen remains awkwardly placed for the remainder of the game. Still, 9...♛d8 is not very appetizing either."

10.	♗b3		0-0
11.	♖ad1		♗d6
12.	♖fe1		♗xf4
13.	♕xf4		♘b6
14.	♖d3		♘bd5

Black is attempting to bring more pieces to the kingside as White is clearly gearing up for a strong attack.

15.	♕h4		♘e7
16.	♘g3		♘g6
17.	♕g5		h6
18.	♕d2		♗d7

Black has succeeded in shoring up his kingside with several very accurate moves. White now makes a surprising decision in order to retain some advantage – one that probably would not occur to most of us. What is it?

19. ♘ce4!   **...**

The decision of an experienced master! As Kmoch notes, "...the endgame, after 19...♕xd2 20. ♘xf6+ gxf6 21. ♖xd2 f5 22. ♘h5, favors White. Still, Black ought to take it on as the middlegame is perilous for him." Indeed, I believe it was essential for Levy to trade queens, although even in 1965 facing Walter Shipman in a long, difficult endgame was a thankless task. What Levy does here, chessically, is "jumping out of the frying pan into the fire."

19. ...   **♘d5?**
20. c3   **♕a5?**

Although 20...♕e7 was imperative, after 20. ♘c5 (threatening 21. ♘f5) Black's position is terrible. What now follows is a wonderful combination and a terrific example of *removing the guard...* but for what square? See if you can figure it out.

21. ♗xd5!!   **exd5**

Kmoch points out that, "21...cxd5 makes no difference; and, on 21...♕xd5, White gets the same continuation after 24. c4! ♕xc4 (forced)."

| 22. ♘f6+! | gxf6 |
| 23. ♕xh6 | ... |

And now you know what dark square White needs to conquer!

| 23. ... | ♖fe8(?) |

If 23...♗g4 24. h3 ♕c7, aiming for a possible queen trade (25. hxg4? ♕f4!), then White is forced to find 25. ♖f3! ♗xf3 26. ♘f5 and mate is inescapable.

| 24. ♖f1! | 1-0 |

For if 24...♗g4, then 25. f3 ♕c7 26. fxg4 either forces mate or wins Black's queen for a knight.

Supplemental Game

A trenchant example of the problems Black might face if he plays 6...♗f5 in this variation.

36. Scandinavian Defense
L. Kristol – T. Morozova
USSR 1966

---

1. e4 d5 2. exd5 ♕xd5 3. ♘c3 ♕a5 4. d4 ♘f6 5. ♗c4 c6 6. ♘ge2(!) ♗f5 7. 0-0 e6 8. ♘g3 ♗g6 9. ♕e2 ♗e7 10. f4! ♕d8 (10...0-0?? 11. f5 and White wins a bishop) **11. f5 exf5 12. ♘xf5 ♗xf5 13. ♖xf5 ♕xd4+??** (An astonishingly greedy mistake! As Black will lose the right to castle and is way behind in development, this is simply suicidal. Black had to play 13...0-0, when after 14. ♗e3 ♘bd7 15. ♖af1 ♘b6 16. ♗d3 ♘bd5, I believe White, with her two bishops and greater central control, is clearly better, or, as IM Jovanka Houska opines in her *Starting Out: The Scandinavian* (Everyman Chess, 2009), "Black's position remains very solid." You decide.) **14. ♗e3 ♛d7 15. ♗c5 ♚f8** (forced) **16. ♖d1 ♗xc5+ 17. ♖xc5 ♛c7** (Notice White has five pieces developed against Black's two, plus Black has forfeited castling – certainly these advantages are worth much more than one pawn.) **18. ♖e5 ♘a6 19. ♖e1 b5** (Can you ignore Black's threat? See below):

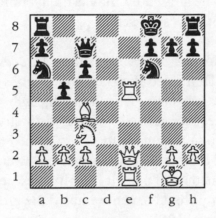

20. ♖e7! (Yes, one last time, *by making a bigger one!)* **20... ♛b6+ 21. ♔h1 bxc4 22.♛xc4 ♘d5 23. ♘xd5 ♛b5** ("Please trade queens," but really, what should you do?):

24. ♘f6!	1-0

Mate in two cannot be stopped. 24. ♘c7! is the same thing. A cautionary tale!

I find it oddly appropriate that the last game in this book was played almost two hundred years before the first one! This should further reinforce the notion that the basic attacking concepts I am advocating have been used by the best players for several centuries, and have not been superseded.

Ercole del Rio was of the so-called *Modenese masters* – the other two being Domenico Ponziani and Giambatista Lolli – who were the best Italian players in the eighteenth century, del Rio clearly being the strongest. He had a distinctly active, combinational style, quite the opposite of his great French contemporary Philidor, who promoted a somewhat slower, "grinding" and pawn-grabbing method of play. It is a pity they never met over the board – it certainly would have resembled the great Tal-Botvinnik matches of 1960 and 1961.

In the following game you will see just how acute del Rio's understanding of the "tenderness" of f2 and f7 was, and also when the vulnerability of these squares was more *apparent* than *real!*

37. Giuoco Piano
Giambattista Lolli – Ercole del Rio
Modena 1755

1. e4	e5
2. ♘f3	♘c6
3. ♗c4	♘f6
4. ♘c3(?)	...

168

Allowing the *fork trick* (4...♘xe4! 5. ♘xe4 d5), which gives Black complete equality (or perhaps even a tiny edge). If White wants to avoid the Two Knights' Defense he should play 4. d3. Of course, Black's reply here is also perfectly OK.

4. ...	♗c5
5. ♘g5?	0-0
6. a3?!	...

If this move were played by one of my post-beginner adult or younger students, I would first congratulate them for trying to preserve their light-squared bishop from a possible ...♘a5. But hopefully by now *you* understand that here it is just plain time-wasting and silly. Still, it allows del Rio to set one of the most amazing traps I have ever seen!! By playing what?

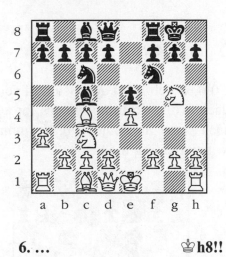

| 6. ... | ♔h8!! |

What the heck?! Well, had Lolli thought it through he should have played 7. d3, although after 7...♕e7 Black is clearly better. Still, who could not resist playing...

| 7. ♘xf7+? | ♖xf7 |

8. ♗xf7   **...**

What now? (P.S. You should have had the next move and its follow-up already prepared.)

8. ...   **♛f8!**
9. ♗c4(?)   **...**

Correct is 9. 0-0, which is an admission of complete failure in the opening. Black, with two minor pieces for a rook and pawn, would stand much better and enjoy great winning chances. But what is wrong with retreating the bishop?

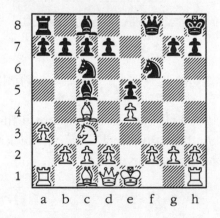

9. ... ♗xf2+!

Please analyze and confirm for yourself that 10. ♔xf2?? ♘xe4+ is a forced mate in seven.

10. ♔f1 **d5!**

Threatening 11...♘g4 with an irresistible attack down the f-file. *Never be afraid to shed pawns during an attack!*

11. ♗e2	**dxe4**
12. d3	**♗h4**
13. ♔g1	**♕c5+!**
14. d4	**♘xd4**
15. ♗e3	**♘f3+**
16. ♔f1	**...**

Everything loses.

16. ...	**♕xe3**
17. ♕d8+	**...**

Hope springs eternal. The idea is to vacate d1 for his knight. Note that both 17. g3?? and 17. gxf3?? allow 17...♗h3#!.

17. ...	**♘g8**
18. ♘d1	**...**

Finish with a flourish! You can do it!

18. ...	♕g1+!
19. ♖xg1	♘xh2#

What a beautiful and strangely little-known game; truly first class all the way. May it inspire you to do likewise!

In an interview in the June 2011 issue of the British magazine *Chess* (p. 37), retired GM Michael Stean was asked the following question about *Simple Chess,* his masterpiece on positional chess for the intermediate player (Faber & Faber, 1978; reprinted by Dover Publications, Inc., in algebraic notation in 2002):

"How did you come up with the idea of writing *Simple Chess,* a book which hasn't really dated?"

His response was:

"Simple Chess *was written with a view to try and articulate – as best I could – the things that I wanted answers to when I was reading chess books but the answers weren't there. Subsequently I discovered – having joined a mainstream profession (tax accountant) – that when you go through training, you get the same syndrome, in that the classical text books give you a lot of information but never in the form of telling you what you actually need to know."*

I hope that with *Simple Attacking Plans* I, too, have helped you begin to learn "what you actually need to know."

So… get cracking!

Fred Wilson, August 2012

Player Index

(Numbers refer to the games;
boldface indicates player had the white pieces)

Index of Openings

(Numbers refer to the games)